Mathseeds

MATH
skills for First Grade

Sara Leman

Blake
e
LEARNING

Welcome to the Mathseeds Workbook for First Grade!

This workbook covers core math and problem solving skills. The carefully structured sequence of fun, and rewarding lessons ensures everyone succeeds.

This workbook includes 50 lessons, plus 10 quizzes with regular reviews, and rewards. Each lesson teaches a concept with four worksheets and lots of engaging activities to build skills. Research shows that targeting a single skill in each lesson greatly improves long-term retention, builds a deeper understanding of maths concepts, and establishes a strong foundation for lifelong success in math.

We know you'll enjoy learning math with us because

Math + Fun = Mathseeds

By the same team that brought you **Reading Eggs!**

Mathseeds First Grade Workbook

www.mathseeds.com

ISBN: 978-1-74215-339-1

Copyright © 2018 Blake eLearning
Reprint 2021

Distributed by:
Blake eLearning
37 West 26th Street
Suite 201. New York, NY 10010

Written by Sara Leman
Publisher: Katy Pike
Series Editor: Amanda Santamaria
Editors: Kate Mihaljek, Amy Russo, and Megan Smith
Design and layout by Modern Art Production Group
Printed by 1010 Printing International LTD

HOW TO USE THIS BOOK

Mathseeds is a carefully sequenced program of 200 lessons. There are 50 lessons for First Grade that comprehensively cover number, operations, patterns, geometry, and measurement.

The Year Planner on pages vi–x gives an overview of each lesson's learning focus, skills and assessment tools in an easy to follow format. You can see at a glance how this academically-rigorous program comprehensively covers the content for an entire school year.

Lessons

- Each lesson has 4 pages of activities to reinforce learning.

Lesson Review

- At the end of each lesson, the yellow review panel helps track achievement.

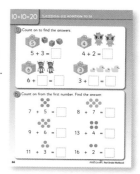 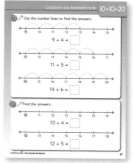  

Color when online lesson is complete.

Complete the name of the pet that hatches at the end of each online leeeson.

Check each new skill to celebrate success.

Driving Tests are part of the online program. Learners can tick them off as they complete them.

I finished this lesson online. 65

This pet hatched.
Tahiti the

I can
- Count on from largest number to add
- Add to 20 using a number line

Driving tests
Tick when complete.
Operations 4, 6, 7 & 12:
Count on
Make 10
Number line addition
True or false?

Quizzes

- Quizzes test knowledge from the previous five lessons and are followed by a reward certificate. Certificates include a checklist to celebrate achievement.

Online Lessons

The workbook lessons can be completed as a stand-alone math program, but when combined with the online lessons, they act as a powerful boost for numeracy success. Best of all, each online lesson is aligned with the workbook, making an integrated approach easy to achieve.

Each online Mathseeds lesson begins with a video of a new math concept, followed by guided practice with activities, games and songs. By following each online lesson with the workbook lesson pages, learners are able to put into practice their new skills and strategies.

Learn with clear and concise instruction videos → **Explore** with interactive online lessons → **Practice** with workbook lessons

CONTENTS

Mathseeds First Grade Workbook

CONTENTS

YEAR PLANNER

Map 11

Lesson	Teaching Focus	Book Pages	Skills	Driving Tests
51	Operations: Addition to 10	2–5	✓ Add three groups on a number line. ✓ Add up to 10 on a number line. ✓ Use an addition equation. ✓ Write a number sentence.	Operations 1 & 2
52	Geometry: Sorting 2D Shapes	6–9	✓ Recognize, name, and sort 2D shapes. ✓ Recognize the difference between straight and curved sides. ✓ Recognize sides and corners.	Geometry 1, 2, 3, 6, 10
53	Operations: Subtraction • Part 2	10–13	✓ Take away and count how many are left. ✓ Fill in subtraction number sentences.	Operations 16, 18, 22, 24
54	Measurement: O'clock	14–17	✓ Recognize the hour hand on an analog clock. ✓ Tell time to the hour on an analog clock. ✓ Show where the minute and hour hands should be to tell time to the hour.	Measurement 1
55	Measurement: Near and far	18–21	✓ Identify things that are near and far. ✓ Remember size and length words.	Measurement 2
End of Map 11 Quiz	Revision	22–23	✓ Addition up to 10 on a number line. ✓ Recognize, name and sort 2D shapes. ✓ Recognize sides and corners. ✓ Subtracting from 10 using strategies. ✓ Tell time to the hour on an analog clock. ✓ Identify things that are near and far.	

Map 12

Lesson	Teaching Focus	Book Pages	Skills	Driving Tests
56	Number: Number lines 11 to 20	26–29	✓ Order numbers 11–20. ✓ Count forward and backward from 11-20. ✓ Use a number line to add.	Number 1
57	Geometry: Position	30–33	✓ Recognize and understand position words. ✓ Follow instructions using position vocabulary.	Kindergarten Geometry 9, 11, 13, 14
58	Operations: Subtract on a number line	34–37	✓ Count back to subtract on a number line. ✓ Write a subtraction equation. ✓ Use a number line to subtract.	Operations 9
59	Measurement: Area	38–41	✓ Understand the concept of area. ✓ Compare the area of different shapes. ✓ Count squares to find area.	Grade 2 Geometry 6
60	Number: Counting 20 to 30	42–45	✓ Name, say, and write the numerals 20–30. ✓ Order numbers from 1–30. ✓ Make and compare numbers in Base Ten Blocks.	Number 1, 2, 3
End of Map 12 Quiz	Revision	46–47	✓ Name, say, and write the numerals 10–30. ✓ Count forward and back. ✓ Follow instructions using position words. ✓ Count back to subtract on a number line. ✓ Count squares to find area.	

Mathseeds First Grade Workbook

Map 13

Lesson	Teaching Focus	Book Pages	Skills	Driving Tests
61	Fractions: Wholes and halves	50–53	✓ Know that halves are two equal pieces. ✓ Identify halves and wholes. ✓ Show one half.	Patterns 3, 5, 6
62	Geometry: 3D Objects • Stack, roll, and slide	54–57	✓ Identify which 3D objects can stack, roll, or slide. ✓ Identify which motion each 3D shape can make. ✓ Recognize that flat faces and curved surfaces make different motions possible.	Geometry 8, 17, 19
63	Number: Ordinal numbers	58–61	✓ Identify ordinal numbers 1st to 10th. ✓ Order the ordinal numbers from 1st to 10th.	Kindergarten Number 24, 25
64	Measurement: Money	62–65	✓ Recognize bills and coins. ✓ Recognize the value of each bill and coin. ✓ Use multiple coins to make amounts. ✓ Add amounts of money together to find a total.	Measurement 3, 5, 6, 7
65	Operations: Addition to 20	66–69	✓ Count on from the largest number to add. ✓ Addition to 20 using a number line. ✓ Addition to 20 using objects.	Operations 4, 6, 7, 12
End of Map 13 Quiz	Revision	70–71	✓ Recognize halves and wholes. ✓ Know that halves are two equal pieces. ✓ Identify which motion each 3D shape can make. ✓ Use ordinal numbers from 1st to 10th. ✓ Identify bills and coins. ✓ Addition to 20 using a number line.	

Map 14

Lesson	Teaching Focus	Book Pages	Skills	Driving Tests
66	Fractions: Halves and fourths	74–77	✓ Know fourths are four equal pieces. ✓ Identify fourths, halves, and wholes. ✓ Show one fourth. ✓ Count the number of equal parts.	Patterns and Fractions 11, 13, 14
67	Number: Counting 30 to 40	78–81	✓ Name, say, and write the numerals 30–40. ✓ Order numbers from 30–40. ✓ Recognize what number is being shown using Base Ten blocks.	Number 4
68	Operations: Find the difference	82–85	✓ Count to find the difference between two groups. ✓ Find the difference between two numbers on a number line. ✓ Link finding the difference to subtraction equations. ✓ Find the difference to solve word problems.	Operations 9
69	Geometry: Put shapes together	86–89	✓ Fit 2D shapes over larger 2D shapes. ✓ Compose 2D shapes to make larger shapes. ✓ Copy a model composed of 3D objects.	Geometry 9, 13
70	Measurement: O'clock and half-past	90–93	✓ Recognize digital time on the hour. ✓ Identify half-past time on analog clocks. ✓ Read times on the hour and half-hour written in words.	Measurement 9, 10
End of Map 14 Quiz	Revision	94–95	✓ Identify halves, and fourths. ✓ Find the difference to solve a subtraction equation. ✓ Name, say, and write the numerals 30–40. ✓ Compose 2D shapes to create a larger shape. ✓ Identify and write digital and analog times to the hour and half hour.	

Map 15

Lesson	Teaching Focus	Book Pages	Skills	Driving Tests
71	Operations: Sharing	98–101	✓ Count to share items into equal groups. ✓ Identify how many items are in each group.	Kindergarten Operations 21
72	Operations: Doubling	102–105	✓ Count and add to make doubles. ✓ Use addition equations to show doubles.	Grade 2 Operations 22
73	Measurement: Heavy and light	106–109	✓ Recognize items which are heavy and light. ✓ Use a balance scale to sort items by weight. ✓ Know that if the scale balances they weigh the same.	
74	Operations: Grouping	110–113	✓ Divide a larger group into smaller, equal groups. ✓ Count out groups of a given number. ✓ Add groups to make a total.	Kindergarten Operations 8
75	Number: Counting 40 to 50	114–117	✓ Name, say, and write the numerals 40–50. ✓ Order and compare numbers from 40–50. ✓ Make and recognize numbers in Base Ten Blocks.	Number 5, 6, 7, 8, 11
End of Map 15 Quiz	Revision	118–119	✓ Count to share items equally between groups. ✓ Count and add to double. ✓ Use a balance scale to sort items by weight. ✓ Add groups to find a total.	

Map 16

Lesson	Teaching Focus	Book Pages	Skills	Driving Tests
76	Operations: The equals sign	126–129	✓ Use the equals sign to show that two sums are equal. ✓ Use the equals sign to mean 'the same as'.	Operations 10, 11
77	Number: Counting by 2s and 5s	130–133	✓ Skip count by 2s and 5s. ✓ Skip count on the number line. ✓ Count groups of 2 and 5 to find a total.	Patterns and Fractions 7, 8
78	Geometry: Position • Left and right	134–137	✓ Identify left and right. ✓ Follow directions using position and movement vocabulary.	Geometry 4, 5
79	Number: Counting by 10s	138–141	✓ Skip count by 10s. ✓ Skip count on the hundred chart. ✓ Skip count on a number line. ✓ Count groups of 10 to find a total.	Patterns and Fractions 9
80	Data: Tallies and graphs	142–145	✓ Read a table of picture data. ✓ Identify categories with the most or least items. ✓ Use tally marks to record and read information. ✓ Read and interpret picture graphs.	Data 1, 2, 3, 9
End of Map 16 Quiz	Revision	146–147	✓ Use the equals sign to show that two sums are equal. ✓ Skip count by 2s, 5s, and 10s. ✓ Recognize left and right. ✓ Use tally marks and answer questions about data.	

Map 17

Lesson	Teaching Focus	Book Pages	Skills	Driving Tests
81	Number: Counting 50 to 70	150–153	✓ Name, say, and write the numerals 50–70. ✓ Order numbers from 50–70.	Number 12
82	Data: Chance	154–157	✓ Identify situations that definitely will or won't happen. ✓ Recognize that some events might happen. ✓ Use the terms more and less likely, possible, and impossible.	Data 5, 7, 11
83	Measurement: Money	158–161	✓ Recognize the value of bills and coins. ✓ Use multiple coins and bills to make amounts. ✓ Add amounts of money to find a total. ✓ Solve word problems with money.	Measurement 12
84	Measurement: Measuring length	162–165	✓ Measure length using uniform units. ✓ Compare lengths based on measurements.	Measurement 4, 13, 14
85	Operations: Find the difference	166–169	✓ Match items and count to find the difference. ✓ Find the difference between two numbers using a number line. ✓ Write subtraction algorithms. ✓ Find the difference to solve a word problem.	
End of Map 17 Quiz	Revision	170–171	✓ Write numbers 50 to 70. ✓ Identify events that will and won't happen. ✓ Measure lengths using uniform units. ✓ Use bills and coins to make amounts. ✓ Find the difference between two numbers to 20.	

Map 18

Lesson	Teaching Focus	Book Pages	Skills	Driving Tests
86	Number: Counting 70 to 100	174–177	✓ Name, say, and write the numerals 70–100. ✓ Order numbers from 70–100. ✓ Compare numbers from 1–100.	Number 13, 15, 16
87	Measurement: Half-past and digital clocks	178–181	✓ Read and identify half-past times on digital clocks. ✓ Match digital and analog clocks. ✓ Add one hour to a time.	Measurement 8, 15
88	Base Ten: Trading tens	182–185	✓ Trade 10 ones blocks for a ten stick. ✓ Trade ones for tens when adding. ✓ Make a ten when adding two numbers. ✓ Use trading to solve word problems.	Number 9, 10
89	Measurement: Capacity	186–189	✓ Measure capacity in informal units. ✓ Use smaller containers to measure the capacity of larger containers. ✓ Identify which containers are best for measuring capacity.	Measurement 11, 17, 18, 19
90	Number: Skip counting patterns	190–193	✓ Skip count by 2s and 5s using a number line. ✓ Identify the missing numbers in patterns by counting by 2s and 5s. ✓ Make number patterns on the hundred chart. ✓ Use skip counting to solve word problems.	Patterns and Fractions 10, 12
End of Map 18 Quiz	Revision	194–195	✓ Read analog clocks and write digital half-hour times. ✓ Add one hour to digital times. ✓ Count numbers 70 to 100. ✓ Order the capacity of containers. ✓ Trade 10 blocks for a ten stick when adding. ✓ Count by 2s and 5s.	

Map 19

Lesson	Teaching Focus	Book Pages	Skills	Driving Tests
91	Operations: Near doubles	198–201	✓ Identify near doubles. ✓ Know the doubles of numbers 1–10. ✓ Double the smaller number and add 1 or 2.	
92	Measurement: Change from $20	202–205	✓ Understand the concept of change. ✓ Calculate change on a number line. ✓ Calculate change from $10 or $20.	
93	Operations: Number fact families	206–209	✓ Recognize related pairs of addition and subtraction sums. ✓ Identify number fact families consisting of four related sums. ✓ Use number fact families to complete equations.	Number 16
94	Geometry: Position	210–213	✓ Use position vocabulary. ✓ Identify clockwise and counterclockwise turns. ✓ Follow directions.	Geometry 11, 12, 15
95	Operations: Add 2 digits to 1 digit	214–217	✓ Add 1 digit numbers to 2 digit numbers. ✓ Split numbers into tens and ones to add. ✓ Count on from the larger number on a number line. ✓ Count on using a hundreds chart. ✓ Use addition strategies to solve word problems.	Number 13, 15
End of Map 19 Quiz	Revision	218–219	✓ Use near doubles to add. ✓ Subtract to find the change from $10 and $20. ✓ Use number fact families to write sums. ✓ Follow directions. ✓ Use addition strategies to add 2 digits to 1 digit.	

Map 20

Lesson	Teaching Focus	Book Pages	Skills	Driving Tests
96	Operations: Bridging to 10	222–225	✓ Bridge to a 10, then add the difference. ✓ Use a number line or hundred chart to bridge to 10. ✓ Solve word problems using the bridge to 10 strategy.	Operations 18
97	Data: Tallies and graphs	226–229	✓ Equate tally marks with numerals. ✓ Fill a picture graph to match given data. ✓ Use a picture graph to answer questions.	Data 10, 12, 15, 16
98	Base Ten: Add and subtract tens	230–233	✓ Add and take away a group of tens. ✓ Use a number line to add or subtract tens. ✓ Use a hundred chart to add or subtract tens. ✓ Solve word problems to 100.	Operations 17, 19, 20
99	Geometry: 3D Objects - Prisms	234–237	✓ Identify prisms amongst other objects. ✓ Understand that prisms have identical end faces and rectangular faces. ✓ Draw different types of prisms.	Geometry 7, 18
100	Operations: Subtracting unknown numbers	238–241	✓ Find the number to be taken away in a subtraction sum. ✓ Use ten frames, number mountains, and number lines to find unknown numbers when subtracting. ✓ Solve word problems finding unknown numbers.	Operations 8
End of Map 20 Quiz	Revision	242–243	✓ Bridge to a ten and add the difference. ✓ Use a strategy to add a group of tens. ✓ Use a data table to answer questions. ✓ Recognize square prisms, triangular prisms, and rectangular prisms. ✓ Use a strategy to find an unknown number when subtracting.	

Number

Hand Prints

Make sets of hand prints and cut them out. Use ten pairs and label the pairs in multiples of ten to 100. Make the hand prints into a wall chart.

Patterns

Eye Spy

Practice counting in twos by counting eyes of different groups of people, animals, or toys. Use estimation before counting. *"How many eyes do you think are in your toy box?"*

Fractions

Halves and Fourths

Make up a sheet with the outline of rectangles, squares, circles, and triangles. Make sure you have lots of colored pencils. Read out instructions like, *"Color one fourth of your rectangle green. Color half of your triangle blue."* Continue until all of the shapes are colored.

Gobble

Provide a slice of bread and a plastic butter knife. Trace around the bread on a piece of paper. Now, cut the bread in half and draw a corresponding line on the outline. Next cut the bread into fourths and draw another line. Now, gobble some of the bread! Color in the gobbled fourths and work out how much was eaten—one or three fourths, one half, or the whole slice.

Operations

Treasure Hunt

This game is best played outdoors. Create doubles dot pattern cards and hide them outdoors. Count to 10 then use chalk to write down the numbers 1–5 down on the pavement. Set a time limit to race around and find the matching double card in the garden. Draw the doubles dot pattern alongside the numbers 1–5 and fill in the equation □ + □ = □.

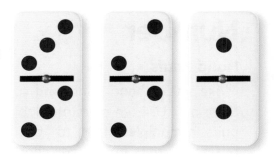

Counting Caterpillar

Label 10 paper plates with 10s to 100. Have one more paper plate to act as the head of the caterpillar. Put the head of the caterpillar and the rest of the plates on the floor in a muddled order. Count by 10s and position the plates correctly. Once all of the plates are in order, use them to count forward and backward by tens. Turn some over. "*Which ones are missing? Connect the plates with string and hang up for practice.*"

Money

Shopping

Collect a group of play bills and coins and review their values. Look at an online catalog of a favorite retailer. You could link this with a family event or upcoming holiday. Take turns to be shopkeeper and customer. The customer chooses an item and works out which bills and coins they will use. The shopkeeper takes their money and gives them any change needed. Then swap roles and go again.

Time

When is it?

At the beginning of a day, take time to write a schedule of activities. Divide a large piece of paper into hour and half-hour blocks and write in the plan. For example: 8:00—walk the dog, 9:00—reading and writing, 11:00—fruit snack, 11:30—math, 1:00—lunch, 2:00—art, 2:30—library, 4:00—baseball practice. Watch the clock throughout the day and when the time comes to change the activity use a musical instrument or special sign to signal activity change.

Measurement

Which Hat?

Place three hats on the floor with the labels lighter, heavier, and the same. Put out an object to be the comparison item, such as an apple. Have a set of items which are lighter, heavier, and the same weight as the object. Choose which hat it must go in. Allow hefting of items or provide a balance scale to help with estimating.

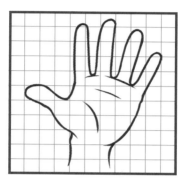

Trace it

Trace around hands on grid paper and count the squares to find the area. Do the same with feet or shoes. Use a large sheet of paper and trace around the outside of your body. Discuss what could be used to measure these larger areas (sheets of paper for example) and choose units to measure the area with. Explore with larger and smaller areas. *"Do different sizes work better for different body parts?"*

Geometry

Feely Bag

Collect a variety of 2D shapes and a small bag. Put one shape in at a time and ask questions about what the shape feels like, and to identify the faces. *"Is it 2D or 3D? How many vertices can you feel?"*

Collage

Provide a large piece of card and lots of shapes cut out of colored paper— triangles, squares, rectangles, half circles. Explore composing larger, recognizable shapes using two or more of the coloured shapes. Talk about shapes which work well together and those that don't. Be sure to label each shape with its name when the picture is done.

Build it!

You'll need two players for this activity. Select a stack of colored building blocks and erect a barrier between the two players. One player builds with their blocks while describing their movements to the other, who tries to copy them. At the end, see if you have the same structure. Swap roles and go again

1 ✏️ Count and add.

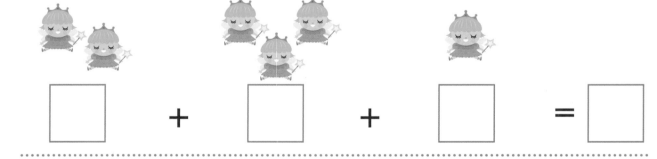

2 Count. ✏️ Write the numbers. Find the total.

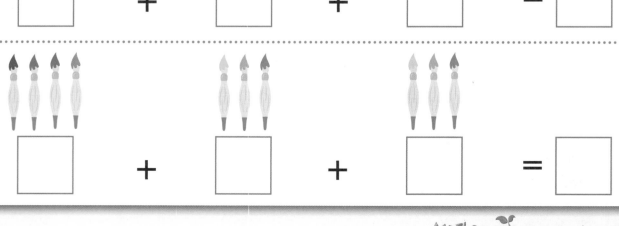

③ ✏️ Add Mango's fruit together.

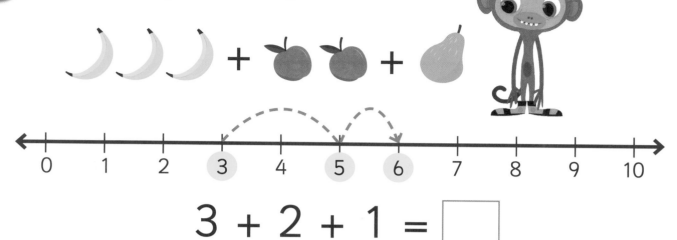

$3 + 2 + 1 =$ ⬜

④ ✏️ Use the number lines to find the answers.

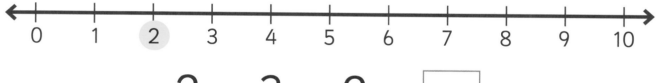

$2 + 3 + 2 =$ ⬜

$4 + 2 + 4 =$ ⬜

$1 + 3 + 5 =$ ⬜

⑤ 🖊 Complete the number sentences.

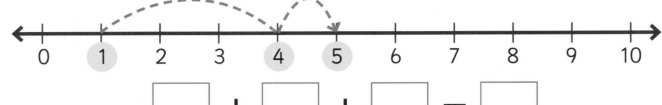

☐ + ☐ + ☐ = ☐

☐ + ☐ + ☐ = ☐

☐ + ☐ + ☐ = ☐

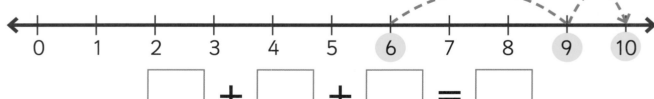

☐ + ☐ + ☐ = ☐

☐ + ☐ + ☐ = ☐

Mathseeds First Grade Workbook

6 ✏️ Find the answers.

1 + 5 + 2 = ☐   5 + 3 + 1 = ☐

2 + 4 + 2 = ☐   4 + 5 + 1 = ☐

7 ✏️ Find the missing numbers.

3 + 3 + ☐ = 7   5 + 2 + ☐ = 10

1 + 1 + ☐ = 5   4 + 2 + ☐ = 8

8 Mango sees 4 white cats, 3 orange cats, and 2 black cats.

How many cats altogether?

✏️ Draw a picture.

✏️ Write a number sentence.

How many cats altogether? ☐

I finished this lesson online.	This pet hatched.	I can	Driving tests
 51	Andy the ☐ 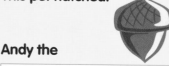	• Add 3 groups on a number line ☐ • Add to 10 on a number line ☐ • Use an addition equation ☐	Tick when complete. Operations 1, 2: 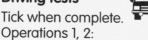 Add to 10 ☐ Add 3 numbers ☐

1 Color the shapes.

triangle = **red**
square = **green**
rectangle = **yellow**
circle = **orange**

2 Match.

1 side

2 sides

3 sides

4 sides

Mathseeds First Grade Workbook

③ ✂ Cut out the shapes on page 251.
Paste them in the correct box.

0 corners	4 sides the same length 4 corners

3 sides 3 corners	2 long sides 2 short sides

4 ✏️ Label the parts of the shapes—**corner** or **side**.

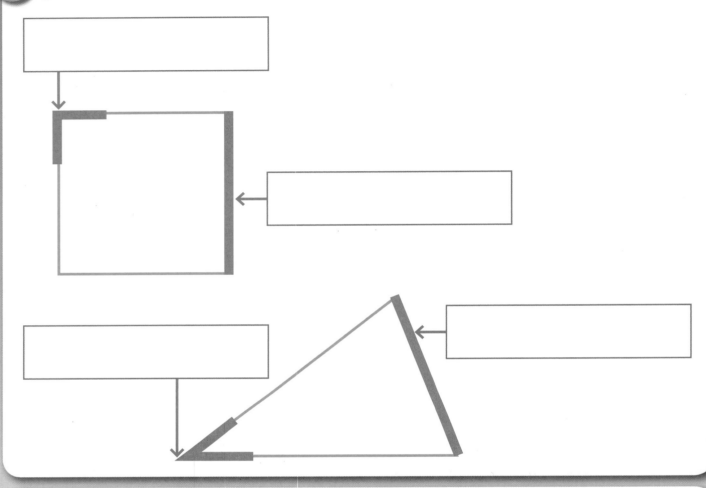

5 ✏️ Draw

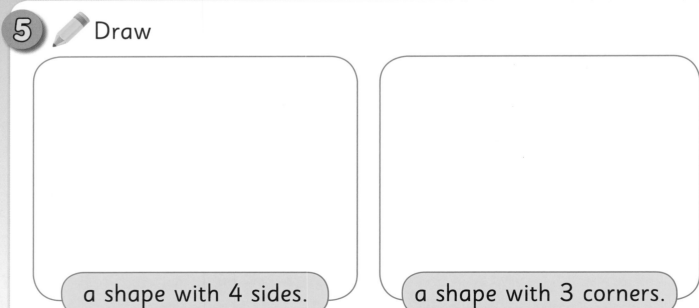

a shape with 4 sides.

a shape with 3 corners.

Mathseeds First Grade Workbook

6 ✏️ Join each shape to the correct jar.

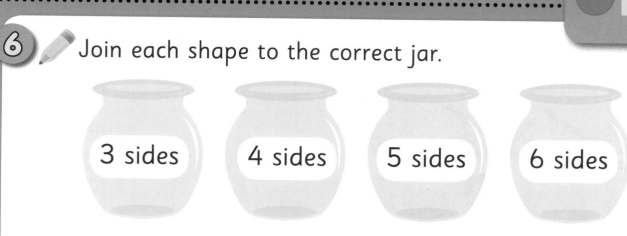

| 3 sides | 4 sides | 5 sides | 6 sides |

7 Read the clues. ✏️ Write the shape name.

I have 4 sides the same length and 4 corners.

I am a _____ .

I have 0 corners.

I am a _____ .

I have 3 sides and 3 corners.

I am a _____ .

I have 2 long sides, 2 short sides, and 4 corners.

I am a _____ .

square

triangle

rectangle

circle

I finished this lesson online.	This pet hatched.	I can	Driving tests
	Justin the _____	• Recognize and name 2D shapes ☐ • Sort 2D shapes by their sides and corners ☐	Tick when complete. Geometry 1, 2, 3, 6, 10: 2D Corners Sides Name 2D shapes Defining 2D

 First Grade Workbook

9

1 ✏️ Complete.

6 take away 2 is

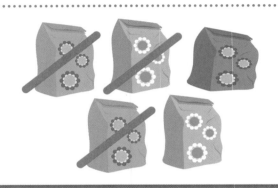

5 take away 3 is

2 Find the answers.

10 − 5 =

5 − 1 =

4 − 3 =

7 − 3 =

Mathseeds First Grade Workbook

③ 🖉 Complete the subtraction sentences.

$\boxed{} - \boxed{2} = \boxed{}$

$\boxed{} - \boxed{3} = \boxed{}$

$\boxed{5} - \boxed{} = \boxed{}$

$\boxed{9} - \boxed{} = \boxed{}$

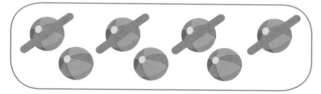

$\boxed{} - \boxed{} = \boxed{}$

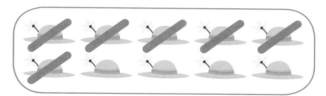
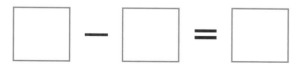

$\boxed{} - \boxed{} = \boxed{}$

④ Cover up with your hand. 🖉 Write the answers.

$6 \quad - \quad 3 \quad = \boxed{}$

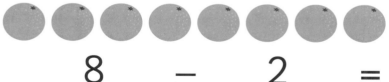

$8 \quad - \quad 2 \quad = \boxed{}$

5 Use your hand to cover up. ✏ Write the answer.

Cover 5 eggs.
How many left? ☐

Cover 3 pots.
How many left? ☐

Cover 4 pencils.

$10 - 4 =$ ☐

Cover 1 orange.

$8 - 1 =$ ☐

6 ✏ Complete the number sentences.

Take away 3.

☐ – ☐ = ☐

Take away 4.

☐ – ☐ = ☐

Mathseeds First Grade Workbook

Subtraction

7 🖉 Write the sums.

$10 - \boxed{} = \boxed{}$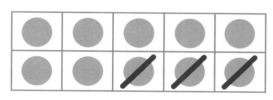

$10 - \boxed{} = \boxed{}$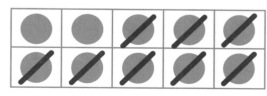

$10 - \boxed{} = \boxed{}$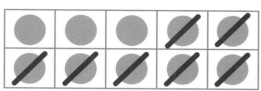

8 🖉 Draw 5 mice. 3 run away. How many left?

$\boxed{} - \boxed{} = \boxed{}$

🖉 Draw 8 cats. 3 hide. How many left?

$\boxed{} - \boxed{} = \boxed{}$

| I finished this lesson online.  | This pet hatched.   Swoop the _____ | **I can** • Take away and count to find how many are left ☐ • Complete subtraction number sentences ☐ | **Driving tests** Tick when complete. 🚗 Kindergarten Operations 16, 18, 22, 24: Subtraction to 5 ☐ Take away to 5 ☐ Subtraction sums to 5 ☐ Subtract to 5 |

1

The long hand is called the minute hand.

It points to 12 when it's an o'clock time.

The time is ☐ o'clock.

2 ✏️ Write the missing numbers. Color the long hand **red**.
The short hand tells the hour. Color the short hand **green**.

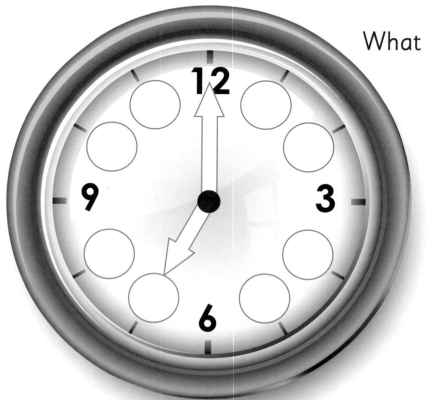

What time is it?

It is ☐ o'clock.

Mathseeds First Grade Workbook

③ What is the time?

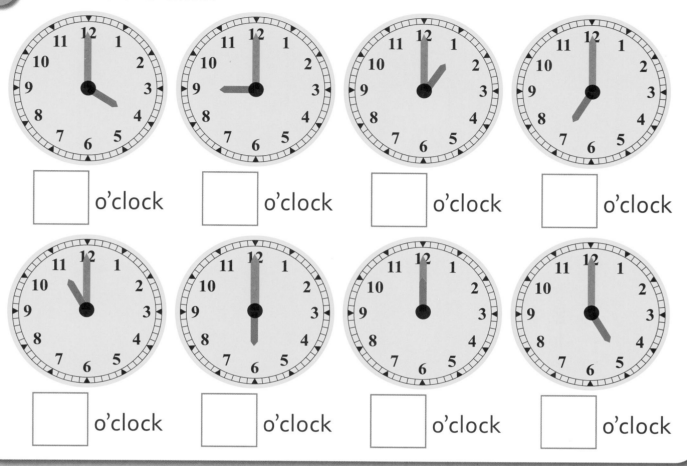

☐ o'clock ☐ o'clock ☐ o'clock ☐ o'clock

☐ o'clock ☐ o'clock ☐ o'clock ☐ o'clock

④ 🖊 Draw the short hand to show the time.

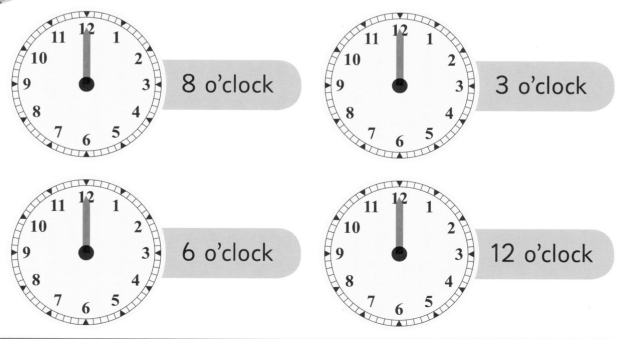

8 o'clock

3 o'clock

6 o'clock

12 o'clock

5 Complete Doc's schedule.

MONDAY		
	6 o'clock	Wake up. 
	☐ o'clock	Eat breakfast. 
	☐ o'clock	Go to the beach. 
	1 o'clock	Eat lunch. 

MONDAY

 | **4** o'clock | Read a book.
 | o'clock | Go to bed.

6 What time does Doc

eat breakfast? _____ o'clock

go to the beach? _____ o'clock

go to bed? _____ o'clock

7 What time do you

wake up? _____ o'clock

eat lunch? _____ o'clock

go to bed? _____ o'clock

| **I finished this lesson online.**  | **This pet hatched.** Sneakers the ☐ | **I can** • Tell time to the hour ☐ • Recognize the hour hand on an analog clock ☐ | **Driving tests** Tick when complete. Measurement 1: O'clock ☐ |

1 (Circle).

Who is near?

Who is far?

2 ✏️ Draw

a cup near the teapot.

a house far away from Ruby.

Mathseeds First Grade Workbook

③ Where is Waldo? Color the correct answer.

near   far

near   far

④ Color the ball closest to Mango **red**.
Color the ball furthest away **blue**.

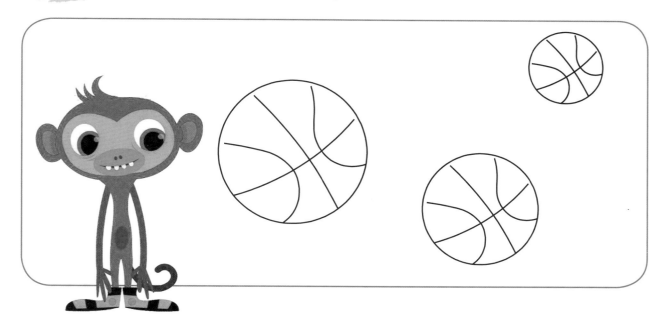

5  Draw

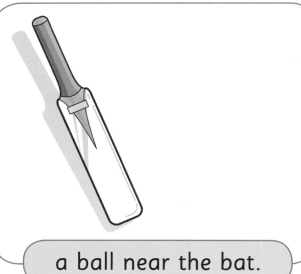

a ball near the bat.

a tree far away from Dizzy.

6 Label each picture with one of these words.

big   tall   long   small   short

7

Color the correct answer. ✕ Cross out the wrong answer.

Which tree is near? (big tree) (small tree)

Which dog is far away? (big dog) (small dog)

Which person is closest? (big person) (small person)

8 Complete the sentences using **big** or **small**.

Things which are far away look _____.

Things which are near look _____.

I finished this lesson online. 	This pet hatched. **Reginald the**	I can • Identify things that are near and far ☐ • Remember size and length words ☐	Driving tests Tick when complete. Measurement 2: Length ☐

1 Use the number lines to find the answers.

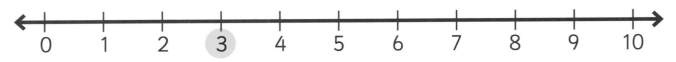

$$3 + 2 + 3 = \boxed{}$$

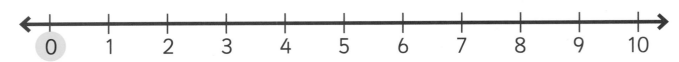

$$0 + 4 + 5 = \boxed{}$$

2 Draw lines to match.

circle	4 corners	4 sides
square	0 corners	3 sides
rectangle	4 corners	1 side
triangle	3 corners	4 sides

Mathseeds First Grade Workbook

3 ✏️ Match each sum to its answer.

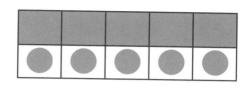

10 – 8

10 – 5

10 – 7

10 – 3

10 – 2

10 – 4

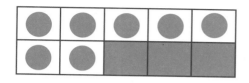

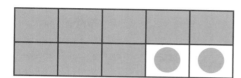

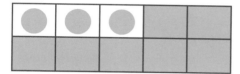

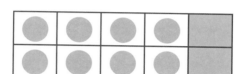

4 What time is it?

 ☐ o'clock

5 ✏️ Draw the missing hand.

 It is 5 o'clock.

6 Color the correct label.

near   far

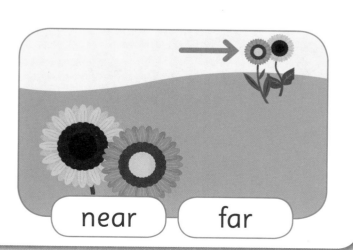

near   far

Fantastic!

YOU COMPLETED

MAP 11

YOU CAN:

- [ ] **Add** three groups on a **number line**.
- [ ] Name **2D shapes** and count their **corners** and **sides**.
- [ ] Complete **subtraction equations**.
- [ ] Tell **time** to the hour.
- [ ] Identify things that are **near** and **far**.

Signed:

_____

Dated:

Mathseeds First Grade Workbook

1 ✏️ Track each time to its matching clock.

3 o'clock

5 o'clock

8 o'clock

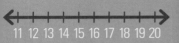
1 🖊️ Match each picture to its number.

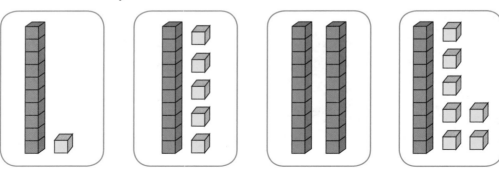

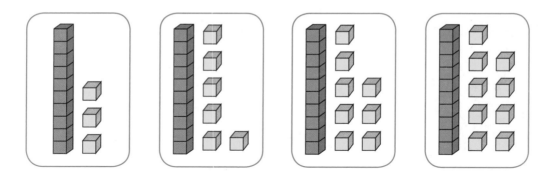

2 🖊️ Complete the number lines.

Mathseeds First Grade Workbook

③ 🖉 Join the pieces to make number lines.

10 11 12   **16 17 18**

15 16 17   **13 14 15**

13 14 15   **18 19 20**

④ Count forward 4 places. Circle the number.

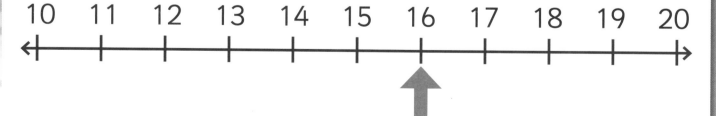

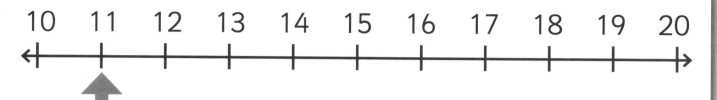

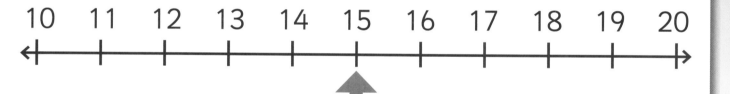

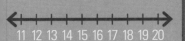
5 Order the numbers. ✏ Write in the bubbles.

◯ ◯ ◯   ◯ ◯ ◯

13 12 11   15 14 16

◯ ◯ ◯ ◯

17 20 19 18

6 Count backward 4 places. (Circle) the number.

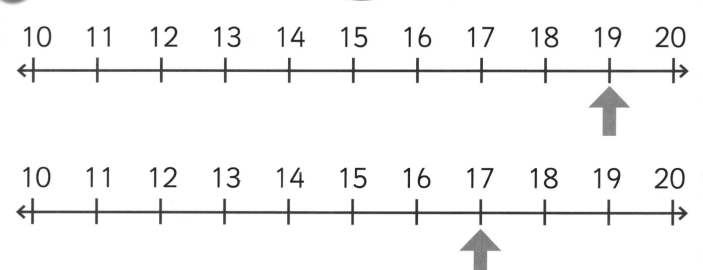

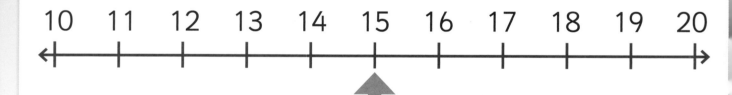

Mathseeds First Grade Workbook

11 12 13 14 15 16 17 18 19 20

7 Which number is

before 12? ☐ before 14? ☐ before 20? ☐

after 17? ☐ after 11? ☐ after 13? ☐

8 ✏️ Write the missing number in each row.

| **20** | | **18** | **17** |

| **14** | **13** | | **11** |

9 Start at 11.
Count on 3.

Write your number. ☐

10 Start at 19.
Count back 3.

Write your number. ☐

1 Match each word to a picture.

on top

next to

between

under

above

behind

in front

inside

Mathseeds First Grade Workbook

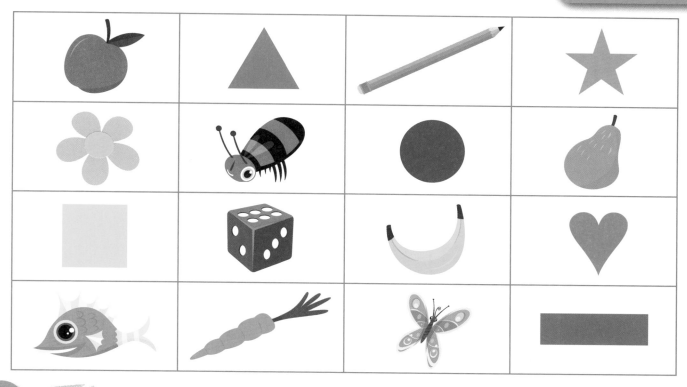

2 Color the answer. Which item is:

above the circle ?

left of the carrot ?

below the apple ?

right of the banana ?

between the triangle and the star ?

above the rectangle ?

③ ✏️ Draw

- a fishbowl **on** the table.

- a cat **in front of** the sofa.

- a ball **under** the table.

- a picture **above** the sofa.

- a balloon **between** the table and the door.

- a book **on** the rug.

4 ✏️ Draw

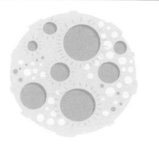

a star below
the moon.

a bird above
the water.

5 Color

the flower **closest** to Ruby red.

the flower **furthest** away blue.

the **smallest** flower yellow.

the **tallest** flower green.

the **biggest** flower purple.

I finished this lesson online.	This pet hatched.	I can	Driving tests
	**Gaston the**	• Recognize and understand position words • Follow instructions	Tick when complete. 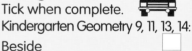 Kindergarten Geometry 9, 11, 13, 14: Beside Above and below In front and behind Far away and near

1 Match each sum to its number line.

7 – 3 = 4

5 – 2 = 3

10 – 4 = 6

8 – 6 = 2

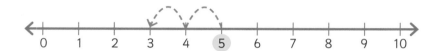

2 Hop back 3 places. ✏️ Write the answer.

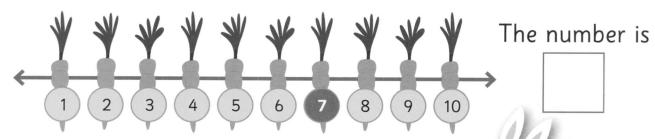

The number is

Hop back 8 places. ✏️ Write the answer.

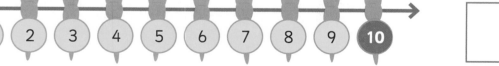

The number is

Mathseeds First Grade Workbook

3 (Circle) the number of stars.

Cross out 3. Jump back to show how many are left: ☐

4 (Circle) the number of hearts.

Cross out 5. Jump back to show how many are left: ☐

5 (Circle) the number of cars.

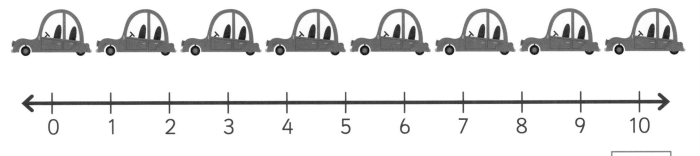

Cross out 4. Jump back to show how many are left: ☐

6 Trace the hops. Answer the sums.

$$8 - 3 = \boxed{}$$

$$6 - 2 = \boxed{}$$

$$10 - 5 = \boxed{}$$

$$9 - 6 = \boxed{}$$

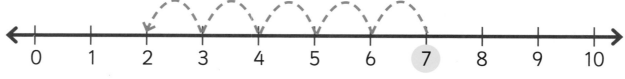

$$7 - 5 = \boxed{}$$

Mathseeds First Grade Workbook

7 Jump along the number line to subtract.

7 – 3 = [ ]

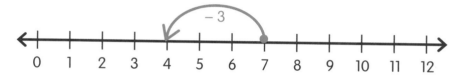

6 – 2 = [ ]

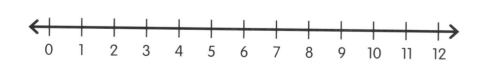

8 – 4 = [ ]

9 – 3 = [ ]

10 – 6 = [ ]

8 ✏ Write the number sentence.

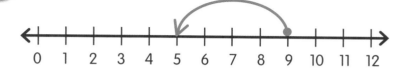 [ ] – [ ] = [ ]

I finished this lesson online.

58

This pet hatched.

Angel the [ ]

I can
- Count back to subtract [ ]
- Use a number line to subtract [ ]

Driving tests
Tick when complete.
Operations 9:
Number line subtraction [ ]

1 (Circle)

the biggest picture.

the smallest picture.

2 Color

the bigger footprint in each pair.

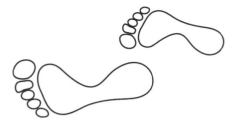

the smaller footprint in each pair.

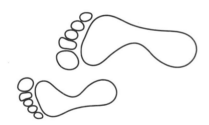

③ Count the squares. ✏️ Write the total for each shape.

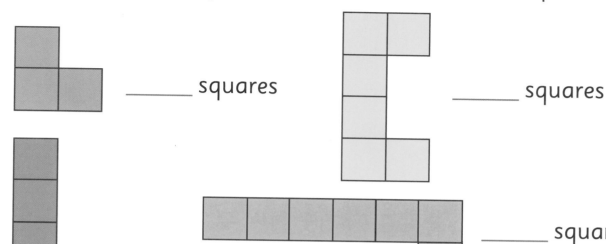

_____ squares

_____ squares

_____ squares

_____ squares

(Circle) the shape that has the largest area.

④ ✏️ Draw and color

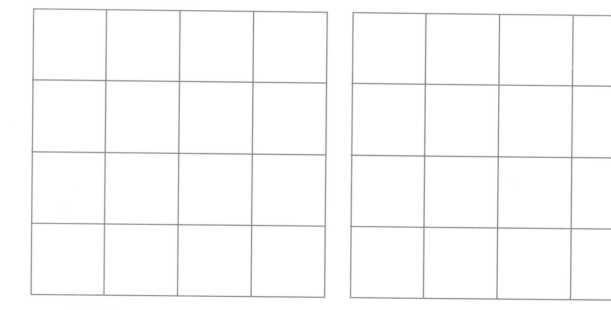

a shape that covers
6 squares.

a shape that covers
12 squares.

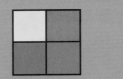
5 (Circle) the one that takes up more space.

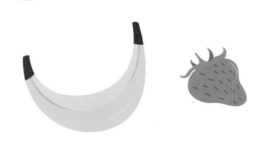

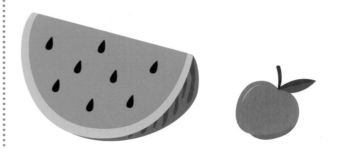

6 How many squares?

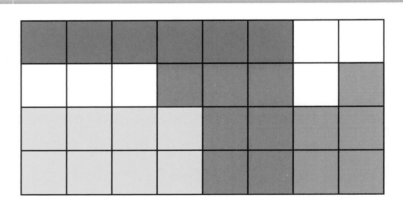

- **green** shape: _____ squares
- **yellow** shape: _____ squares
- **orange** shape: _____ squares
- **purple** shape: _____ squares
- Which shape is largest? _____
- Which shape is smallest? _____

(7) ✏️ Draw around your hand.

How many squares does your hand cover? ☐

(8) Now draw around your foot.

How many squares does your foot cover? ☐

(9) Which is larger? _____

I finished this lesson online.

(59)

This pet hatched.

Helena the

☐

I can
- Compare the areas of different shapes ☐
- Count squares to find area ☐

Driving tests
Tick when complete. 🚗
Grade 2 Measurement 6:
Length and area ☐

1 ✏️ Match.

thirty	**20**	
	21	twenty-three
twenty-five	**22**	
	23	twenty-six
twenty-nine	**24**	
	25	twenty-one
twenty	**26**	
	27	twenty-eight
twenty-two	**28**	
	29	twenty-four
twenty-seven	**30**	

2 Complete the number lines.

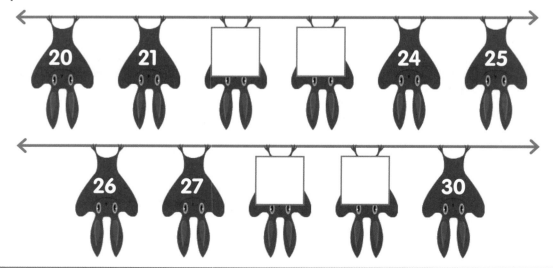

20 21 ☐ ☐ 24 25

26 27 ☐ ☐ 30

Counting 20 to 30

3 Order the numbers. ✏ Write in the bubbles.

22 20 21   24 23 25

30 27 29 26 28

4 Join the beads together to make number lines.

24 25 26   27 26 25

30 29 28   23 24 25

20 21 22   27 28 29

5 ✏ Write
one more than.

21   29   27   24

one less than.

23   26   21   28

6 ✏️ Match the numbers to their names.

twenty-three   **21**   **22**   twenty-four

twenty-two   **23**   **24**   twenty-one

7 ✏️ Write the missing numbers.

24, ☐ , 26   21, ☐ , 23

30, ☐ , 28   27, ☐ , 25

8 ✏️ Match.

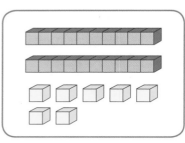

25

26

27

28

29

30

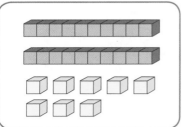

twenty-six

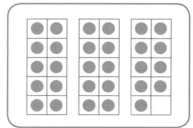

twenty-five

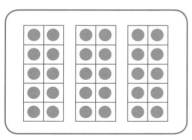

Mathseeds First Grade Workbook

⑨ Write the numbers. Color the larger number.

I finished this lesson online.

60

This pet hatched.

Dougie the

I can
• Recognize numbers 20 to 30
• Order numbers 20 to 30

Driving tests
Tick when complete.
Number 1, 2, 3:
Number lines to 20
Numbers to 30
Sequences to 30

1 🖉 Write the missing numbers.

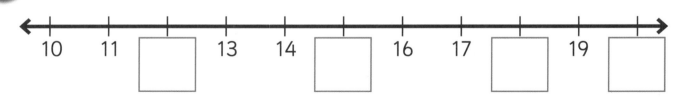

10   11   ☐   13   14   ☐   16   17   ☐   19   ☐

2 Start at 13.
Count on 4.

Write your number. ☐

3 Start at 17.
Count back 5.

Write your number. ☐

4 🖉 Draw

- ● **above** the ★.

- ■ **below** the ★.

- ▲ **next to** the ■.

- ■ **above** the ▲.

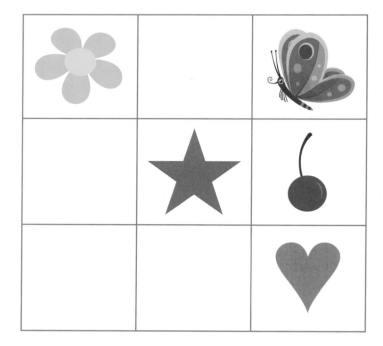

Mathseeds First Grade Workbook

5 Count back. Answer the sums.

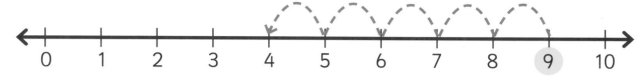

$$9 - 5 = \boxed{}$$

$$10 - 7 = \boxed{}$$

6 Draw and color a shape that covers 15 squares.

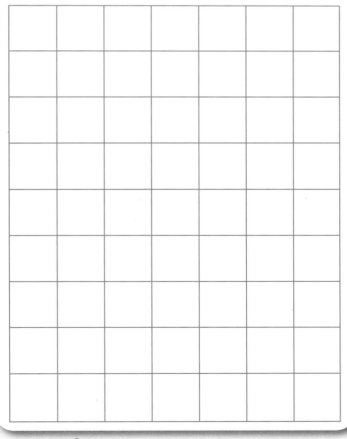

7 Order the numbers. Write in the boxes.

Mathseeds First Grade Workbook

Well done!

YOU COMPLETED

MAP 12

YOU CAN:

- [ ] Count forward and backward **11** to **20**.
- [ ] Recognize and understand **position** words.
- [ ] Use a **number line** to **subtract**.
- [ ] Count squares to find **area**.
- [ ] Recognize numbers to **30**.

Signed:

_____

Dated:

1. ✏️ Join the dots. Color the picture.

1 ✏️ Join Mango to the things that are whole.

2 Circle the foods that have been cut in half.

Mathseeds First Grade Workbook

3 Color the halves in **red** and the wholes in **blue**.

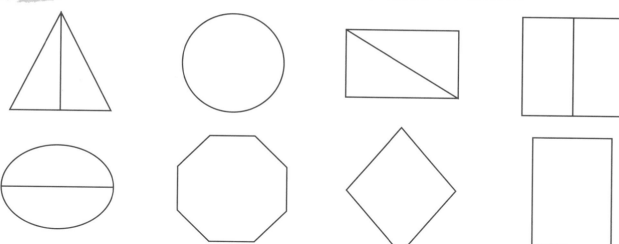

4 ✂ Cut out the pictures on page 251. Paste the matching halves.

5 Paste half of each fruit.

6 Color one half of each item.

7 ✏️ Draw

a whole banana.

a half-full glass of milk.

8 🖉 Draw a line to cut these foods in half.

9 🖉 Draw a line to cut each shape in half. Color one half.

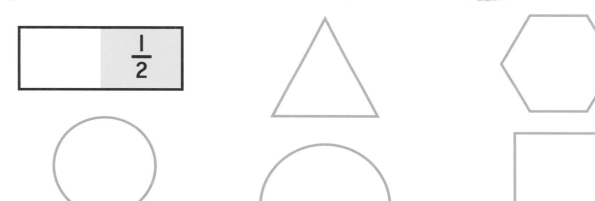

$\frac{1}{2}$

10 Color one half. Make each one different.

a   b   c

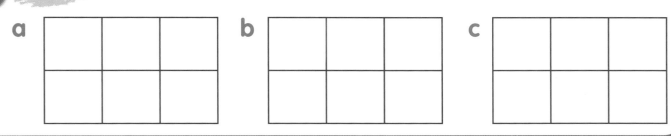

I finished this lesson online.

This pet hatched.

Annie the

I can
- Identify wholes and halves
- Show one half

Driving tests
Tick when complete.
Patterns and Fractions 3, 5, 6:
Halves
Fractions of shapes

1 (Circle) things that are shaped like each 3D object.

 cone

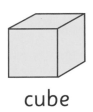 cube

 sphere

2 (Circle) the objects that roll when pushed.

③ (Circle) the objects that slide when pushed.

④ Color **blue** if it rolls, **pink** if it slides, **yellow** if it rolls and slides.

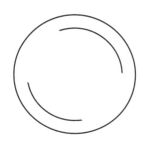
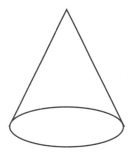
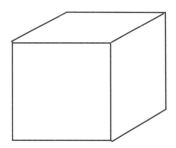

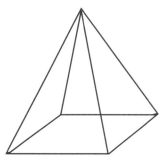
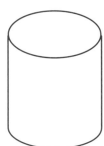
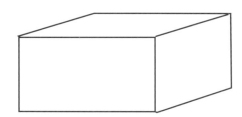

5 ✏️ Draw lines to match.

can stack

cannot stack

6 ✏️ Complete the table. ✓ for yes and ✗ for no.

	can roll	can slide	can stack
⚫			
⬛			
🟫			

7 Color objects that can stack **blue**, yellow if they cannot stack.

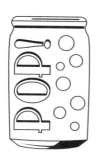
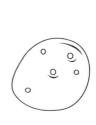

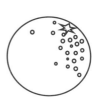
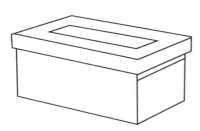

8 🖍 Finish each sentence.

can	roll	stack

Objects with flat faces can _____ .

Objects with curved surfaces can _____ .

Objects with a point on top _____ stack.

I finished this lesson online.

This pet hatched.

Paulo the

I can
• Identify which 3D objects stack, slide or roll

Driving tests
Tick when complete.
Geometry 8, 17, 19:
3D surfaces
3D corners
3D edges

1 Match each word to its number.

first   second   third   fourth   fifth

3rd   **4th**   **1st**   **5th**   **2nd**

8th   **6th**   **10th**   **7th**   **9th**

sixth   seventh   eighth   ninth   tenth

2 Label the cars from 1st to 5th.

FINISH

Color

the first car **red**.   the fourth car **orange**.

the fifth car **yellow**.   the third car **purple**.

the second car **green**.

3 ✂ Cut out the numbers on page 253.
Paste them on the correct prize ribbons.

4 ✏ Write the missing numbers on the stones.

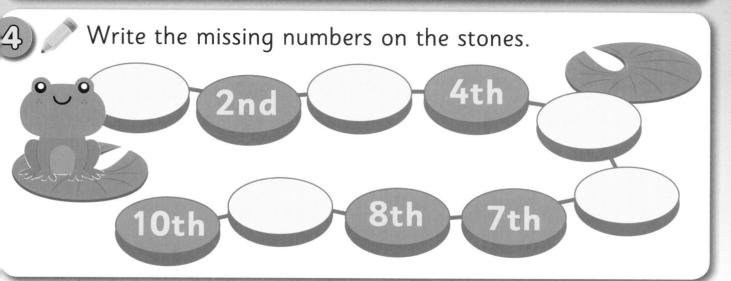

5 Color 3rd and 6th **green**.   2nd and 9th **blue**.
1st and 10th **yellow**.   4th and 8th **orange**.
5th and 7th **red**.

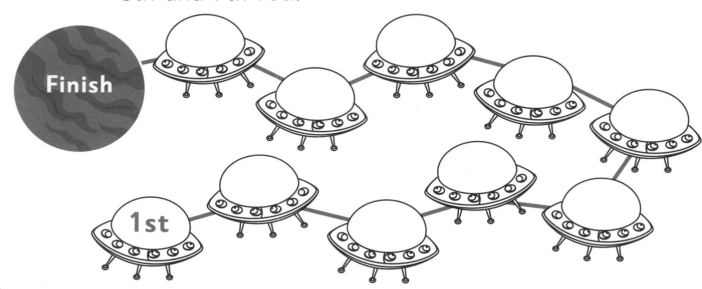

6 Draw a in 4th place.   in 3rd place.

 in 2nd place.   in 1st place.

 in 5th place.

7 ✏ Complete the prizes for the cake contest.

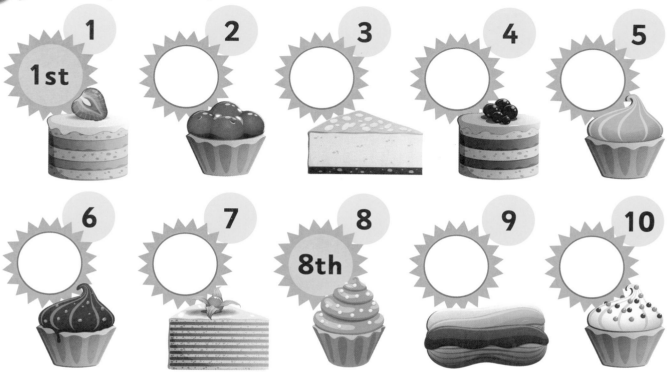

| 1 | 2 | 3 | 4 | 5 |
| 1st | | | | |

| 6 | 7 | 8 | 9 | 10 |
| | | 8th | | |

8 (Circle) the answers.

Which cake came first?

Which cake came last?

Which cake came fourth?

| I finished this lesson online.  | This pet hatched. Hettie the | I can • Recognize ordinal numbers 1st to 10th ☐ • Put ordinal numbers in order ☐ | Driving tests 🚗 Tick when complete. Kindegarten Number 24, 25: Ordinal numbers ☐ Using ordinal numbers ☐ |

1 Color

1¢ coin **orange**.   10¢ coin **red**.

5¢ coin **blue**.   50¢ coin **green**.

25¢ coin **yellow**.

2 Join each item to the correct coin.

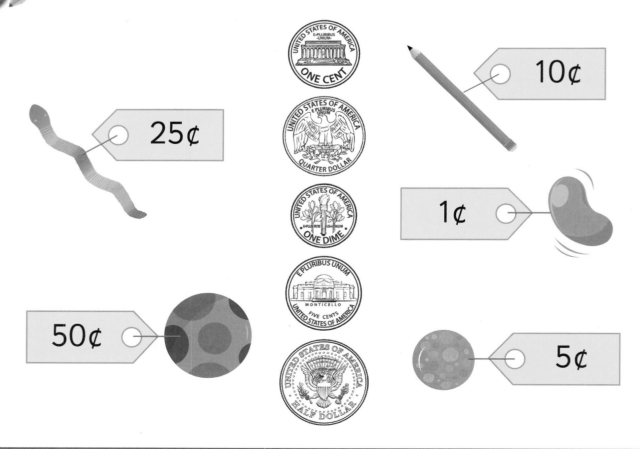

3 ✏ Draw lines to match.

$1

$5

$10

$20

$50

$100

4 ✏ Join each item to the correct bill.

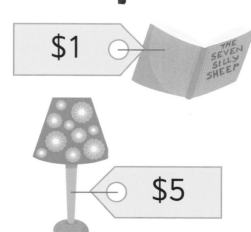

$20

$1

$5

$100

$50

$10

5 Color the most expensive toy **blue** and the cheapest toy **red**.

10¢   50¢

$20 $1

6 How much do they cost altogether? Add to find the answers.

$3   + $1   =   ☐

5¢   +   5¢   =   ☐

$6   + $2   =   ☐

10¢   +   5¢   =   ☐

$10   + $2   =   ☐

Mathseeds First Grade Workbook

7 Color the coins to pay for each thing.

8 How much in each?

¢   ¢   ¢   ¢

I finished this lesson online.	This pet hatched.	I can	Driving tests

I finished this lesson online.

This pet hatched.

Sloop the

I can
- Recognize coins and bills
- Match coins and bills to amounts
- Add coins to make totals

Driving tests
Tick when complete.
Measurement 3, 5, 6, 7:
Coins
Sorting coins
Coin symbols
Identifying coins

1 Count on to find the answers.

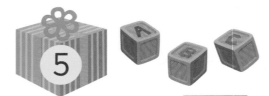

$5 + 3 = \boxed{}$

$4 + 2 = \boxed{}$

$6 + \boxed{} = \boxed{}$

$3 + \boxed{} = \boxed{}$

2 Count on from the first number. Find the answer.

$7 + 5 = \boxed{}$

$8 + 7 = \boxed{}$

$9 + 6 = \boxed{}$

$13 + 4 = \boxed{}$

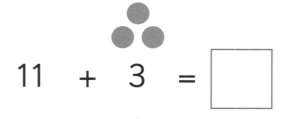

$11 + 3 = \boxed{}$

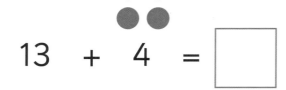

$16 + 2 = \boxed{}$

③ ✏️ Use the number lines to find the answers.

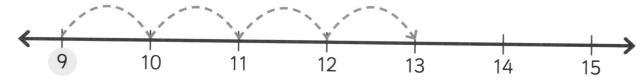

$$9 + 4 = \boxed{}$$

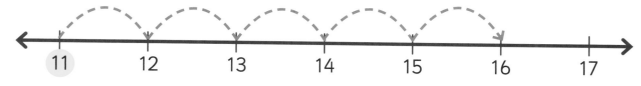

$$11 + 5 = \boxed{}$$

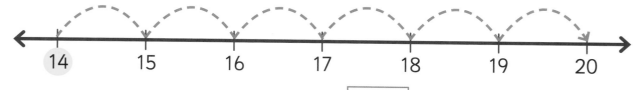

$$14 + 6 = \boxed{}$$

④ ✏️ Find the answers.

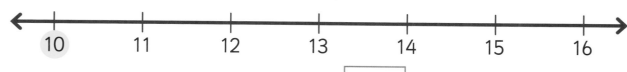

$$10 + 4 = \boxed{}$$

$$12 + 5 = \boxed{}$$

⑤ Count on. Color more squares. ✏ Write the answer.

7	8	9	10	11	12	13	14	15	16

7 + 5 = ☐

11	12	13	14	15	16	17	18	19	20

11 + 5 = ☐

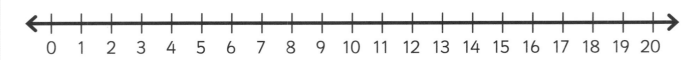

0 1 2 3 4 5 6 7 8 9 10 11 12 13 14 15 16 17 18 19 20

⑥ Count on from the larger number. ✏ Write the answer.

7 + 4 = ☐   8 + 5 = ☐

10 + 2 = ☐   12 + 3 = ☐

14 + 2 = ☐   15 + 4 = ☐

7 Use the number line to help you add.

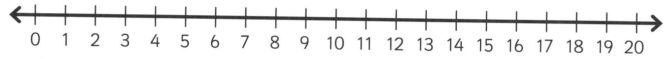

0 1 2 3 4 5 6 7 8 9 10 11 12 13 14 15 16 17 18 19 20

How many insects did each child see?

I saw 6 bees and 5 butterflies. ☐

I saw 8 butterflies and 4 bees. ☐

I saw 10 spiders and 4 flies. ☐

I saw 9 flies and 3 spiders. ☐

I saw 11 grasshoppers and 3 ladybugs. ☐

I saw 8 ladybugs and 6 grasshoppers. ☐

I saw 9 ants and 5 beetles. ☐

I saw 9 beetles and 6 ants. ☐

1 🖊 Match.

whole

half

2 🖊 Draw a line to cut each item in half.

3 Color the words that are true for each object.

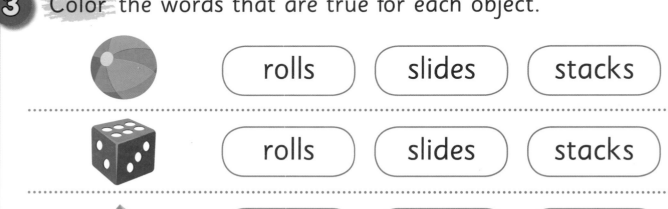

rolls   slides   stacks

rolls   slides   stacks

rolls   slides   stacks

rolls   slides   stacks

Mathseeds First Grade Workbook

4 Color 4th and 6th **green**. 1st and 10th **red**.
5th and 9th **yellow**. 3rd and 7th **purple**.
2nd and 8th **orange**.

FINISH

5 Match.

- THE SEVEN SILLY SHEEP — $10
- 25¢
- $20
- 5¢
- $1
- 10¢

6 Find the answers.

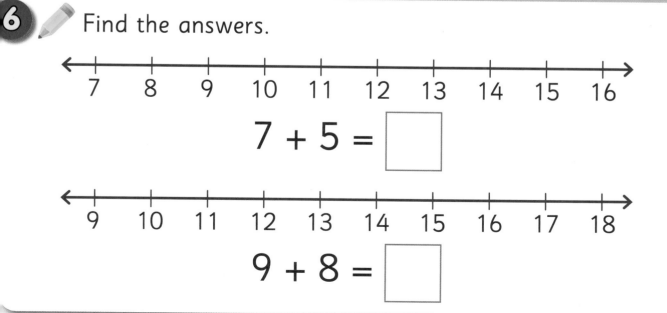

7 + 5 = ☐

9 + 8 = ☐

You're a Star!

YOU COMPLETED

MAP 13

YOU CAN:

- ☐ Recognize **wholes** and **halves**.
- ☐ Identify 3D objects that **roll**, **stack**, and **slide**.
- ☐ Recognize **ordinal numbers 1st to 10th**.
- ☐ Match **coins** and **bills** to amounts.
- ☐ **Add** by counting on using a **number line**.

Signed:

_____

Dated:

Mathseeds First Grade Workbook

1 Draw the other half of the picture.

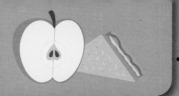

LESSON 66 HALVES AND FOURTHS

1 Match each picture to a word.

half

fourths

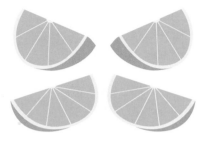

2 Color one half of each shape.

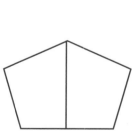

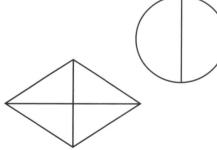

3 Color one fourth of each shape.

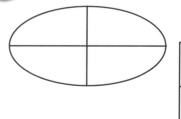

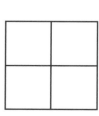

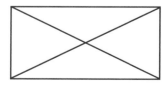

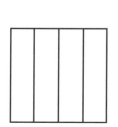

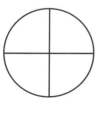

Mathseeds First Grade Workbook

4 Match each fraction to a word.

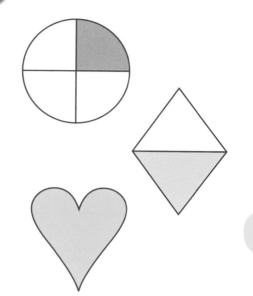

whole

one half

one fourth

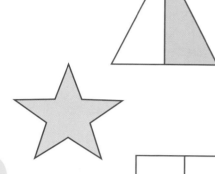

5 Color the shapes divided into fourths **blue** and the halves **yellow**. Remember to look for **equal** parts.

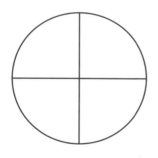
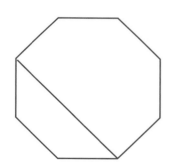
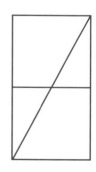
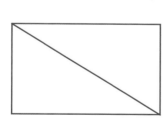

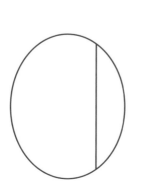
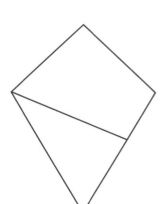
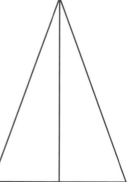
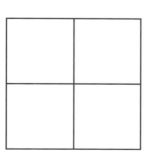

6 Color the items that have been cut into fourths.

7 Draw lines to cut the shape

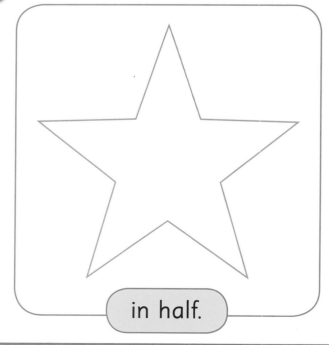

in half.

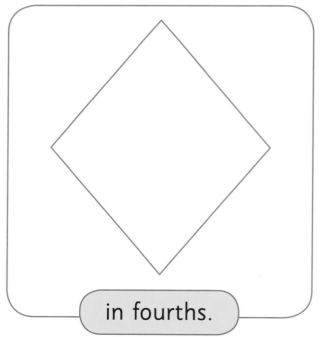

in fourths.

Mathseeds First Grade Workbook

8 Color.

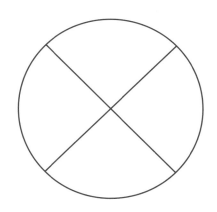
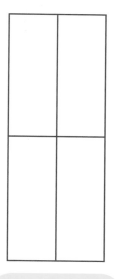
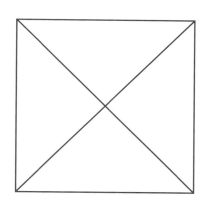

one fourth   one half   one whole

9 (Circle) the shape that has equal parts. How many equal parts?

4 equal parts

☐ equal parts

☐ equal parts

☐ equal parts

I finished this lesson online.	This pet hatched.	I can	Driving tests

I finished this lesson online.

66

This pet hatched.

Lionel the

I can
- Recognize halves and fourths ☐
- Show one fourth ☐
- Count the number of equal parts ☐

Driving tests
Tick when complete.
Patterns and Fractions 11, 13, 14:
Fraction notation ☐
Identify fractions ☐
Calculate fractions ☐

1 ✏️ Write the missing numbers.

30   31   ☐   ☐   ☐

35   ☐   ☐   38   ☐   ☐

2 ✏️ Match the number words and numerals.

thirty-seven

thirty-five

thirty-one

thirty-four

thirty-two

31
34
32
33
38

35
37
30
39
36
40

thirty-three

thirty

thirty-six

forty

thirty-nine

thirty-eight

③ ✏️ Join the berries together to make number lines.

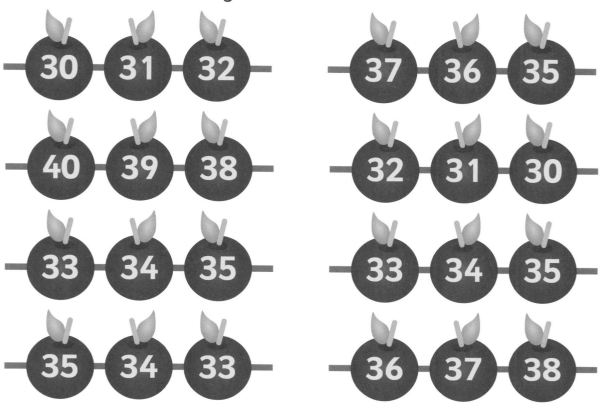

④ ✏️ Order the numbers. Write them in the nests.

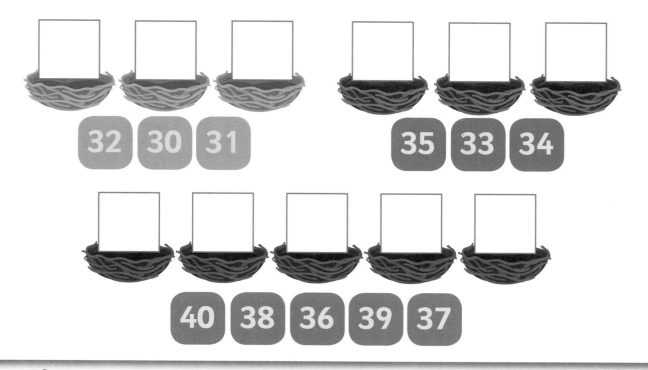

5 ✏️ Match.

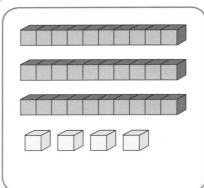 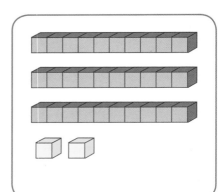 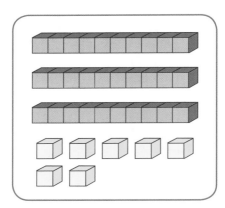

32   **37**   **34**

6 Color the correct number of blocks.

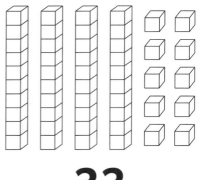 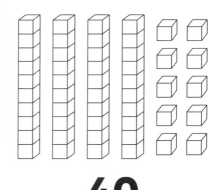 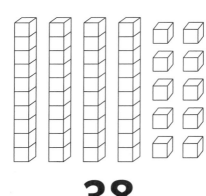

33   **40**   **38**

7 ✏️ Count.

 = 10

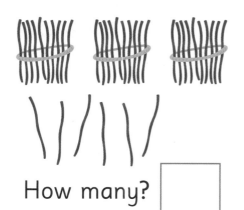

How many? ☐

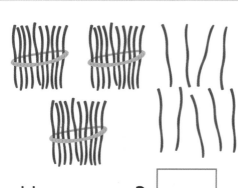

How many? ☐

8 ✏️ Write

one more than.

30 ____   **34** ____   **37** ____   **39** ____

one less than.

31 ____   **33** ____   **36** ____   **38** ____

9 How many tens and ones? ✏️ Write the number.

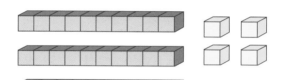

	tens		ones	=	

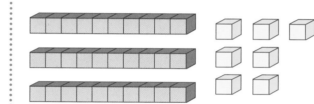

	tens		ones	=	

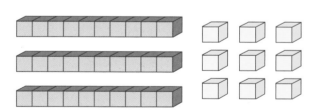

	tens		ones	=	

	tens		ones	=	

I finished this lesson online.

67

This pet hatched.

Mo the

____

I can
- Recognize numbers 30 to 40 ☐
- Order numbers 30 to 40 ☐

Driving tests
Tick when complete.
Number 4:
Order to 40 ☐

1 How many more green fish than orange fish? ☐

$8 - 4 = $ ☐

purple monsters than orange monsters? ☐

$11 - 6 = $ ☐

2 ✏ Find the difference.

The difference between ☐ and ☐ is ☐ .

The difference between ☐ and ☐ is ☐ .

The difference between ☐ and ☐ is ☐ .

3 ✏️ Find the difference.

The difference between 6 and 4 is ☐ .

The difference between 8 and 3 is ☐ .

$9 - 5 =$ ☐

4 Find the difference. ✏️ Write the numbers.

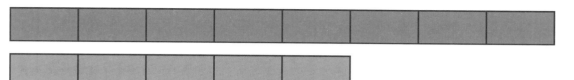

The difference between _____ and _____ is _____ .

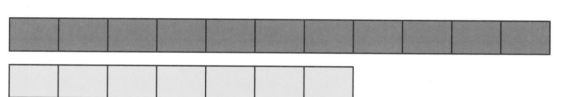

The difference between _____ and _____ is _____ .

5 Count the jumps to find the difference.

The difference between 10 and 4 is ☐

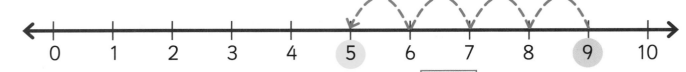

The difference between 9 and 5 is ☐

8 − 4 = ☐

6 Use the number lines to find the difference.

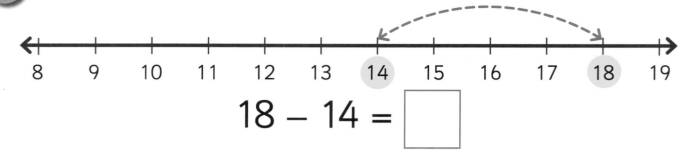

18 − 14 = ☐

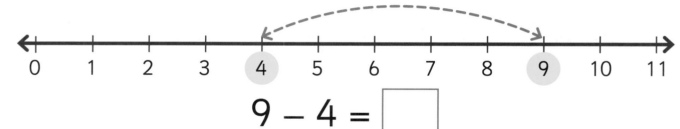

9 − 4 = ☐

Mathseeds First Grade Workbook

7 ✏️ Draw the problems and find the answers.

Mango has 10 pink marbles. Dizzy has 8 blue marbles.
How many more pink marbles are there?

There are ☐ more pink marbles.

Ruby has 9 green bows. Doc has 3 red bows.
How many more green bows are there?

There are ☐ more green bows.

| I finished this lesson online.  | This pet hatched. Lil the _____ | I can • Count to find the difference ☐ • Find the difference using a number line ☐ | Driving tests 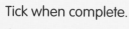 Tick when complete. Operations 9: Number line subtraction ☐ |

1 Each shape has been cut in half. Match.

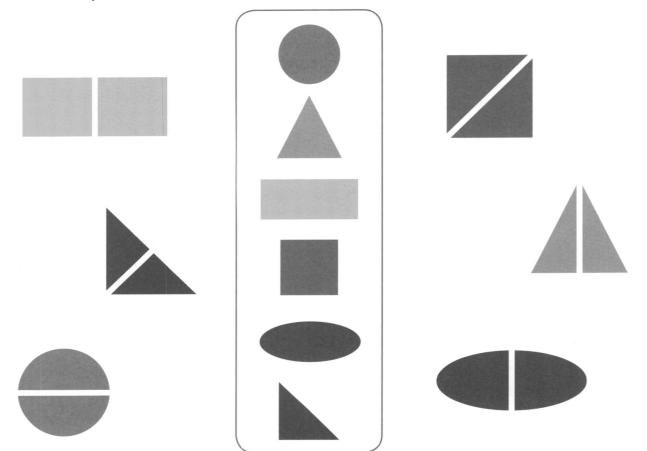

2 ✏️ Draw

2 rectangles to make a square.   4 squares to make a rectangle.

Mathseeds First Grade Workbook

③ ✂ Cut out the shapes on page 253.
Paste them to create new shapes.

Use 4.

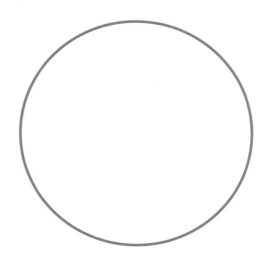

Use 4.

Use 2.

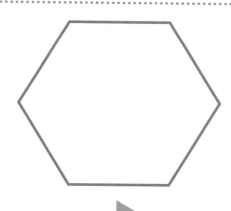

Use 2.

4 Draw 2 lines on each shape to make 4 smaller 2D shapes. Name the shapes you have made.

4 _____   4 _____   4 _____

5 Put together 4 triangles.

What shape did you make? _____

6 Put together 2 half circles.

What shape did you make? _____

7 Color the 3D objects that make each model.

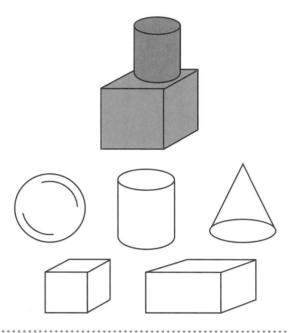

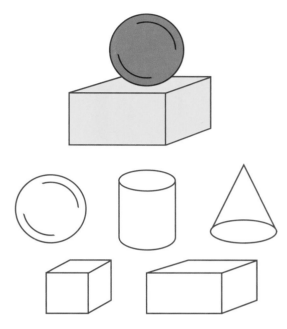

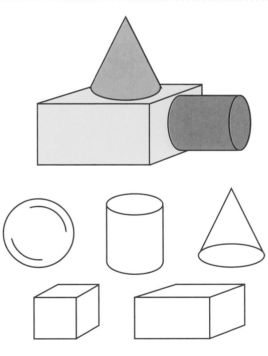

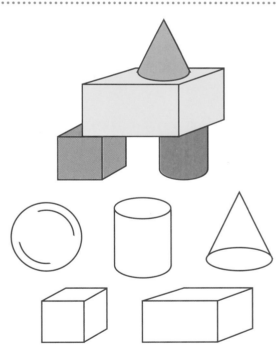

I finished this lesson online.

This pet hatched.

Bobo the

I can
- Fit 2D shapes over larger 2D shapes
- Compose 2D shapes
- Identify 3D objects

Driving tests
Tick when complete.
Geometry 9, 13:
Composing shapes
Composite shapes

 First Grade Workbook

1 ✏️ Match the digital times to the clocks.

4:00

8:00

2:00

10:00

2 ✏️ Write the missing numbers in the digital clocks.

1 o'clock

5 o'clock

9 o'clock

11 o'clock

3 ✏️ What time is it?

It's 10 o'clock. Time to play.

:00

It's _____ o'clock. Time for lunch.

:00

It's _____ o'clock. Time to ride.

:00

It's _____ o'clock. Time for bed.

:00

Mathseeds First Grade Workbook

4 Write in the missing numbers.

Color the big hand **red**.

Color the small hand **green**.

What time is it?

It's half-past ☐ .

5 Draw lines to match.

half-past one

half-past eleven

half-past eight

half-past ten

half-past five

half-past six

Mathseeds First Grade Workbook

6  Draw each minute hand. Write the time.

half-past ☐   half-past ☐   half-past ☐   half-past ☐

7 What time is it?

_____ o'clock   half-past _____   _____ o'clock   half-past _____

_____ o'clock   half-past _____   _____ o'clock   half-past _____

 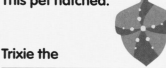

1 ✓ the shapes that show halves.

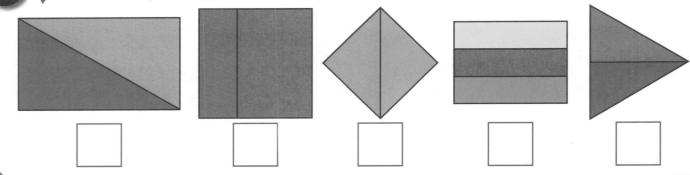

2 Color one fourth of each shape.

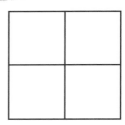 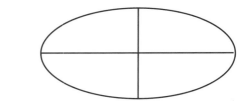 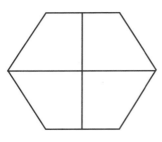

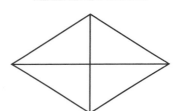  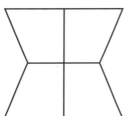

3 ✏ Find the difference.

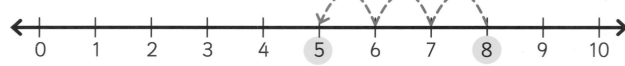

$$8 - 3 = \boxed{}$$

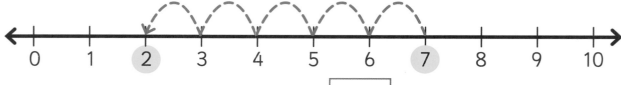

$$7 - 5 = \boxed{}$$

Mathseeds First Grade Workbook

4 Match.

forty	32	31	thirty-seven
thirty-five	34	33	thirty-six
thirty-nine	36	35	thirty-one
thirty-three	38	37	thirty-eight
thirty-two	40	39	thirty-four

5 Draw

4 triangles making a square.

6 Write the digital time.

11 o'clock

7 What time is it?

It is _____

_____

Good Job!

YOU COMPLETED

MAP 14

YOU CAN:

- [ ] Recognize **halves** and **fourths**.
- [ ] Find the **difference** between two numbers.
- [ ] Count and recognize the numbers **30–40**.
- [ ] Compose **2D** shapes.
- [ ] Write **digital** and **analog times** to the hour and half hour.

Signed:

_____

Dated:

Mathseeds First Grade Workbook

1 Crack the code to answer the sums.

🐵 = 1	
🦭 = 2	
🦝 = 3	
🐉 = 4	
🦅 = 5	

🦅 + 🦅 = ☐

🐵 + 🐉 = ☐

🦝 − 🦭 = ☐

🐉 − 🦭 = ☐

2 Color your own pattern of beads.

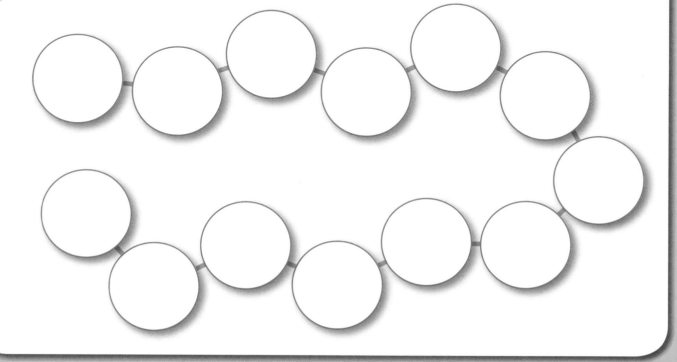

1 ✏️ Draw lines to share the seeds equally between the pots. Write how many seeds in each pot.

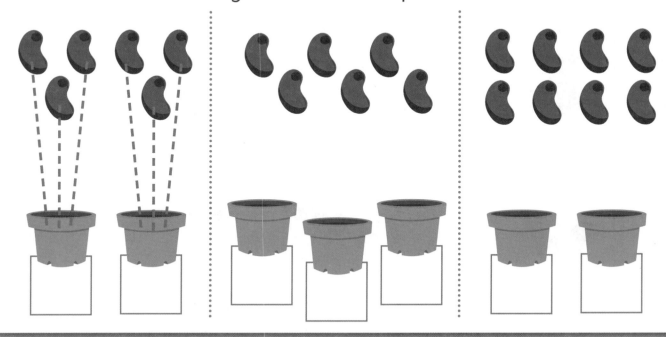

2 (Circle) equal groups to share.

How many carrots each? ▢

How many worms each? ▢

Mathseeds First Grade Workbook

(3) Share equally. ✏ Complete the sentences.

12 bees shared between 3 flowers is ☐ each.

6 candles shared between 2 cakes is ☐ each.

☐ eggs shared between 3 nests is ☐ each.

☐ cookies shared between 2 plates is ☐ each.

4 ✏️ Share equally and complete the number sentences.

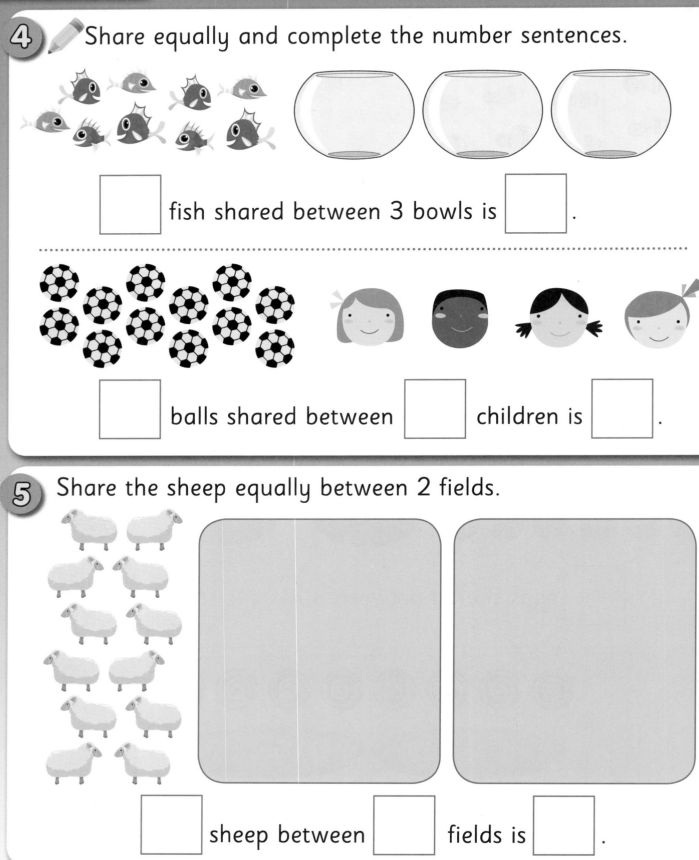

☐ fish shared between 3 bowls is ☐ .

☐ balls shared between ☐ children is ☐ .

5 Share the sheep equally between 2 fields.

☐ sheep between ☐ fields is ☐ .

Mathseeds First Grade Workbook

6 ✏️ Share equally.

□ leaves   □ plates

How many leaves on each plate? □

□ strawberries   □ plates

How many strawberries each? □

I finished this lesson online.

(71)

This pet hatched.

Petra the _____

I can
- Count to share items into equal groups □
- Count how many items are in each group □

Driving tests
Tick when complete.
Kindergarten Operations 21: Sharing □

Mathseeds First Grade Workbook

101

1 ✏️ Write the missing numbers.

 $6 + 6 = \boxed{}$

$\boxed{} + \boxed{} = \boxed{}$

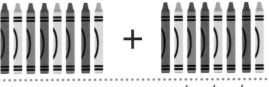 $\boxed{} + \boxed{} = \boxed{}$

 $\boxed{} + \boxed{} = \boxed{}$

$\boxed{} + \boxed{} = \boxed{}$

2 ✏️ Draw matching spots. Write the answer.

Double 6 is $\boxed{}$ Double 8 is $\boxed{}$ Double 7 is $\boxed{}$

(3) Double the number of items. ✏ Write the numbers.

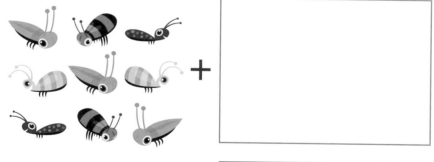 +

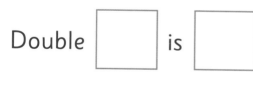 Double ☐ is ☐

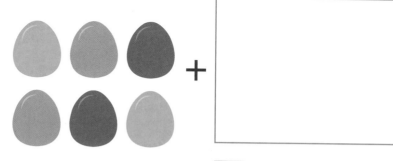 +

 Double ☐ is ☐

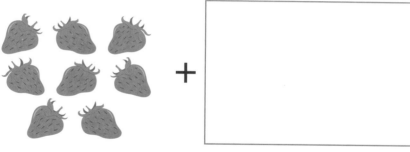 +

 Double ☐ is ☐

 +

Double ☐ is ☐

 +

Double ☐ is ☐

④ ✏️ Write the missing numbers.

 $4 + 4 = \boxed{}$

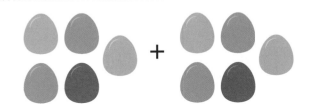 $5 + 5 = \boxed{}$

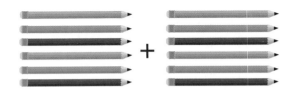 $\boxed{} + 6 = \boxed{}$

 $\boxed{} + \boxed{} = 14$

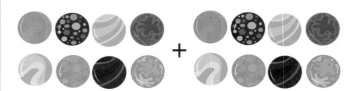 $\boxed{} + \boxed{} = 16$

$9 + \boxed{} = 18$

$\boxed{} + \boxed{} = \boxed{}$

Mathseeds First Grade Workbook

5 ✏ Write the answers.

I double numbers!

6 ✏ Write the answers.

$7 + 7 =$ ☐ $5 + 5 =$ ☐ $9 + 9 =$ ☐

Double 6 is ☐   Double 2 is ☐   Double 10 is ☐

I finished this lesson online.

This pet hatched.

Dennis the ☐

I can
- Add a number to itself to double ☐
- Count and add to double ☐

Driving tests
Tick when complete.
Grade 2 Operations 22: Doubles ☐

Mathseeds First Grade Workbook

105

1 (Circle).

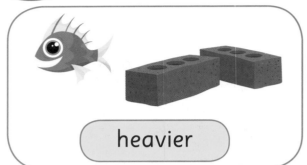

heavier

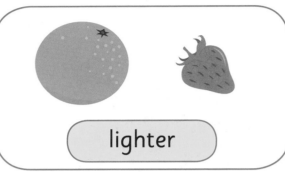

lighter

heaviest

lightest

2 (Circle).

heavier

lighter

heavier

lighter

3 Color the scales that are balanced.

4 Count how many eggs balance each item.

Circle which one is heavier.

5 ✏️ Draw something

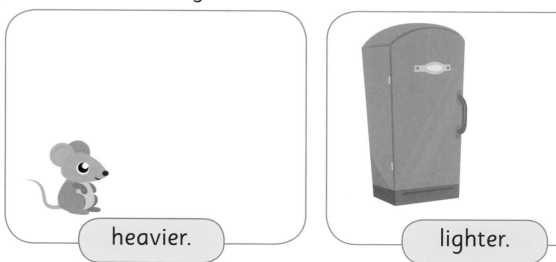

heavier.

lighter.

6 ✂ Cut out the shapes on page 255.
Paste them on the correct side.

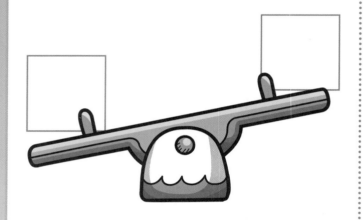

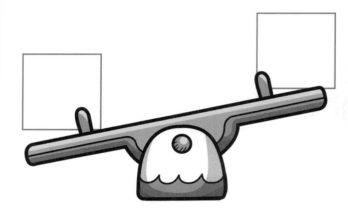

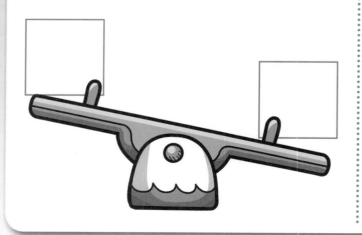

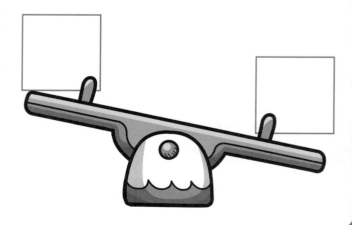

7 ✏️ Match things that weigh the same.

8 ✏️ Draw things on the scales that you think will balance.

I finished this lesson online.	This pet hatched.		I can
73	**Mr. T the** _____	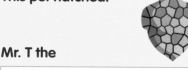	• Identify which items are heavy and light ☐ • Use a balance scale ☐ • Recognize that two items weigh the same ☐

1 Circle

groups of 2.

groups of 3.

groups of 4.

2 Circle groups of 2.

 How many groups?

 How many groups?

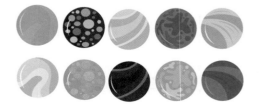 How many groups?

Mathseeds First Grade Workbook

3 (Circle) groups of 3.

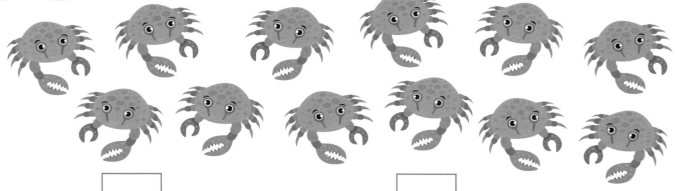

☐ groups of 3 crabs = ☐ altogether

4 (Circle) groups of 2.

☐ groups of 2 berries = ☐ altogether

5 ✏️ Draw.

3 groups of 2 	4 groups of 3

How many 🌼 ? ☐   How many ? ☐

6 Count and write the numbers.

☐ groups of ☐ pencils

☐ groups of ☐ fish.

☐ groups of ☐ doughnuts

☐ groups of ☐ balloons

7 Make 4 groups. Color 5 **red**, 5 **yellow**, 5 **green**, 5 **orange**.

Complete: 4 groups of 5 fish is ☐ altogether.

8 Dizzy counts 8 wheels in a bike shop.
How many bikes can he see?

 Draw a picture.

[ ] groups of [ ] wheels = [ ] bikes altogether

9 Mango sees some sheep in a field.
If there are 20 legs, how many sheep are in the field?

 Draw a picture.

[ ] groups of [ ] legs = [ ] sheep altogether

I finished this lesson online.	This pet hatched.	I can	Driving tests
 **74**	**Brunt the** 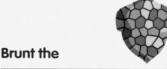	• Divide large groups into smaller, equal groups [ ]	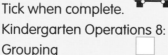 Tick when complete. Kindergarten Operations 8: Grouping [ ]

1 ✏️ Complete the number lines.

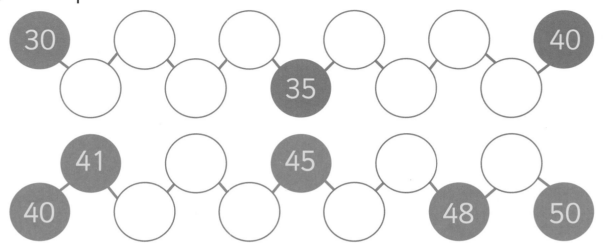

2 ✏️ Join the flags together to make number lines.

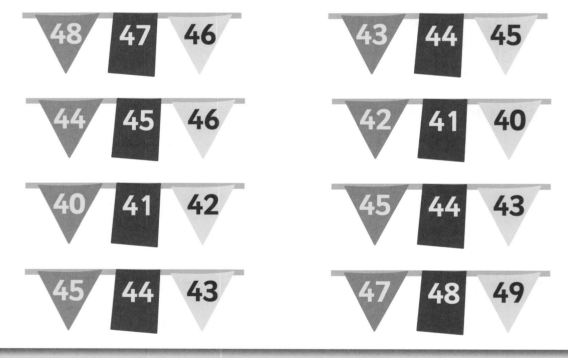

3 ✏️ Write the missing numbers.

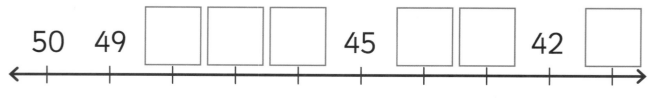

Mathseeds First Grade Workbook

4 Order the numbers. Write them in the clouds.

42 40 41

45 43 44

49 46 47 50 48

5 Write one number before.

| 50 ___ | 41 ___ | 45 ___ |
| 43 ___ | 47 ___ | 48 ___ |

Write one number after.

| 45 ___ | 49 ___ | 40 ___ |
| 42 ___ | 46 ___ | 44 ___ |

6 How many?

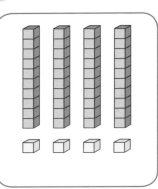 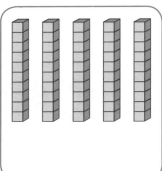 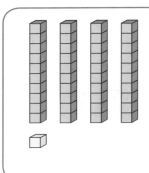 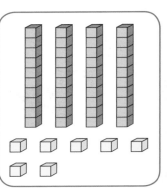

7 Color the correct number of blocks.

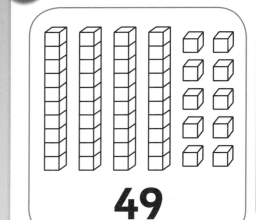

49   **41**   **46**

8 Match.   **46**   **48**   **43**

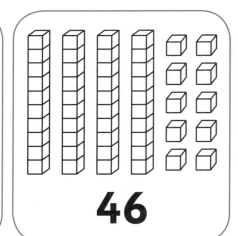

forty-three   forty-six   forty-eight

Counting 40 to 50

⑨ ✏️ Write

two more than.

| 43 | | 45 | | 42 | | 40 | |

two less than.

| 47 | | 50 | | 46 | | 43 | |

⑩ In each group, ~~color~~ the biggest number **yellow** and the smallest number **blue**.

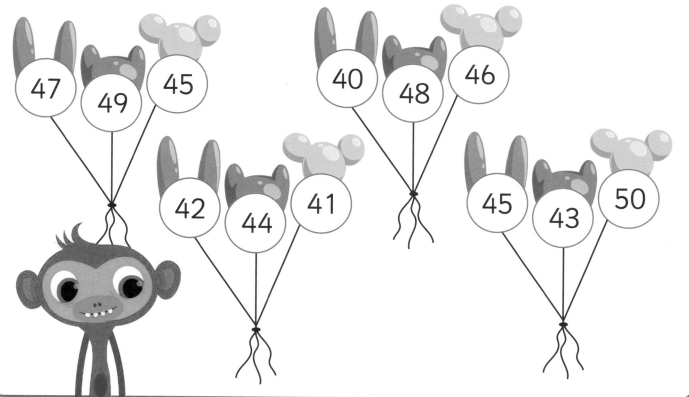

| I finished this lesson online.  | This pet hatched. Shirley the | I can • Recognize numbers 40 to 50 • Order numbers 40 to 50 | Driving tests Tick when complete. Number 5, 6, 7, 8, 11: Count to 50 Number lines to 50 Compare to 50 Count back from 50 |

1 Share equally.

9 bones shared between 3 dogs is ☐ each.

2 ✏️ Write the answers.

 = ☐    = ☐

 = ☐    = ☐

 = ☐    = ☐

☐ + ☐ = ☐   ☐ + ☐ = ☐

3 ✏️ Draw 4 groups of 3 circles ●.

4 groups of 3 = ☐

4 Draw the items on the scales.

5 Share the candles equally.

How many candles on each cake?

 groups of = [ ]   Color each cake.

Hooray!

YOU COMPLETED

MAP 15

YOU CAN:

- [ ] Count to share items into **equal groups**.
- [ ] Count and add to **double to 20**.
- [ ] **Add** groups to find a total.
- [ ] Identify which items are **heavy** and **light**.
- [ ] Recognize and count numbers **40** to **50**.

Signed:

_____

Dated:

Mathseeds First Grade Workbook

1 ✏️ Help everyone find their number word.

15   **20**   36   50   44

fifty   fifteen

forty-four   **twenty**   thirty-six

1 ✏️ Jump along the line to add.

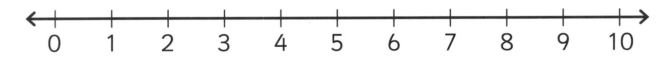

$$2 + 3 + 1 = \boxed{} \qquad 3 + 3 + 2 = \boxed{}$$

$$0 + 4 + 4 = \boxed{} \qquad 4 + 2 + 4 = \boxed{}$$

2 Color the shapes with 3 sides **blue**, 4 sides **yellow**, 5 sides **pink**, and 6 sides **orange**.

3 ✏️ Find the answers.

$$\boxed{5} - \boxed{} = \boxed{} \qquad \boxed{} - \boxed{4} = \boxed{}$$

4 ✏️ Show the time on the clocks.

7 o'clock   **10 o'clock**   **half-past 1**   **half-past 8**

Mathseeds First Grade Workbook

5 Color the starfish **closest to** the crab **green**.

Color the starfish **furthest away** from the crab **purple**.

6 Jump along the line to subtract.

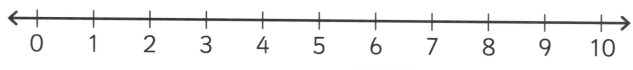

$$10 - 3 = \boxed{}$$

7 Color the shape with the **biggest** area **blue**.

Color the shape with the **smallest** area **yellow**.

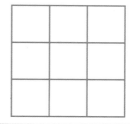 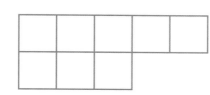 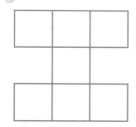

8 Write the numbers. Color the larger number in each pair.

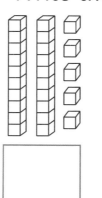 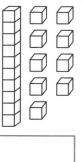 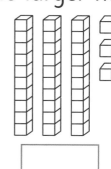 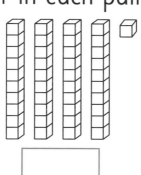

9 Color wholes **red**, halves **yellow**, and fourths **green**.

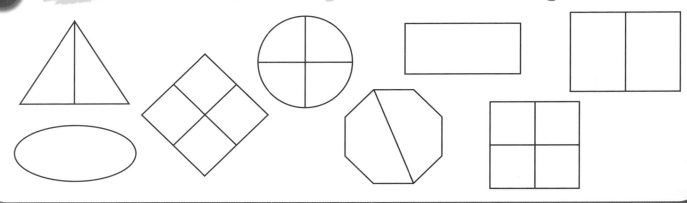

10 Draw something that can

stack. slide. roll.

11 How much?

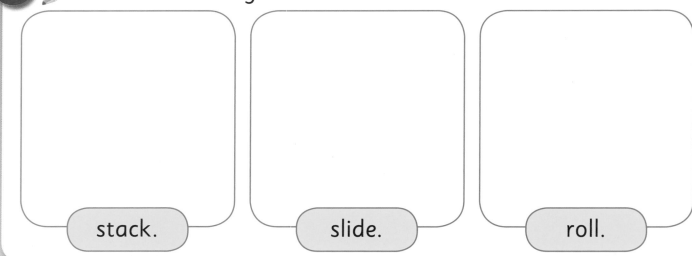

$3 + $2 = [ ]

10¢ + 5¢ = [ ]

$8 + $4 = [ ]

12

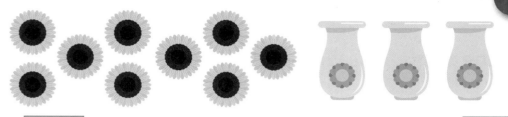

[ ] flowers shared between 3 vases is [ ] .

13 (Circle) groups of 2.

[ ] groups of 2 birds = [ ] altogether.

14 ✏ Write the missing numbers.

36		38		40
	42			45
			49	50

15 Dizzy has 9 red cars. Mango has 4 green cars.
How many more red cars are there?

✏ Draw a picture.

There are [ ] more red cars.

1 ✏️ Write the sums. The first is done for you.

| 4 | + | 4 | = | 8 |

| | | | | |

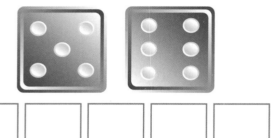

| | | | | |

| | | | | |

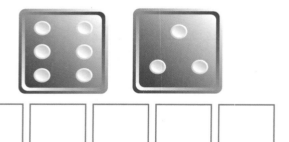

| | | | | |

| | | | | |

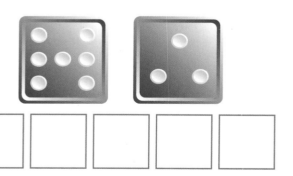

| | | | | |

| | | | | |

2 ✏️ Draw lines to join equal sums.

(3) Are these sums equal? Color yes or no.

$5 + 1 = 3 + 3$

(yes) (no)

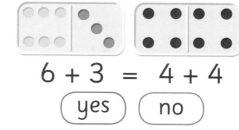

$6 + 3 = 4 + 4$

(yes) (no)

$3 + 4 = 2 + 6$

(yes) (no)

$7 + 3 = 5 + 5$

(yes) (no)

● ● ● ⦸ ⦸ ⦸   ● ● ● ⦸ ⦸ ⦸ ⦸

$7 - 4 \quad = \quad 10 - 7$

(yes) (no)

● ● ● ● ● ● ⦸ ⦸ ⦸   ● ● ● ● ● ● ⦸ ⦸

$9 - 3 \quad = \quad 8 - 2$

(yes) (no)

● ● ● ● ⦸ ⦸ ⦸ ⦸ ⦸ ⦸   ● ● ● ⦸ ⦸

$10 - 6 \quad = \quad 5 - 2$

(yes) (no)

● ● ● ⦸ ⦸ ⦸ ⦸ ⦸   ● ● ● ⦸ ⦸ ⦸ ⦸ ⦸ ⦸

$8 - 5 \quad = \quad 9 - 6$

(yes) (no)

● ● ● ● ● ⦸ ⦸ ⦸ ⦸   ● ● ● ● ● ⦸ ⦸ ⦸ ⦸ ⦸

$9 - 4 \quad = \quad 10 - 5$

(yes) (no)

4 ✏️ Count the blocks. Complete the sums.

$$4 = \boxed{} + \boxed{2}$$

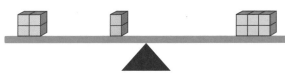

$$\boxed{} + \boxed{} = \boxed{}$$

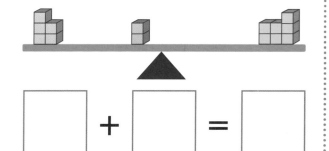

$$\boxed{} + \boxed{} = \boxed{}$$

$$\boxed{} = \boxed{} + \boxed{}$$

5 ✏️ Draw more blocks to make each sum equal.

$$10 = \boxed{} + \boxed{4}$$

$$\boxed{} = \boxed{} + \boxed{}$$

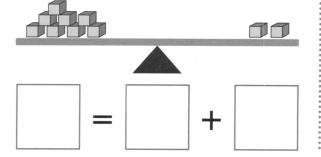

$$\boxed{} = \boxed{} + \boxed{}$$

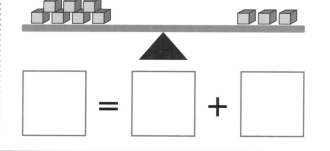

$$\boxed{} = \boxed{} + \boxed{}$$

Mathseeds First Grade Workbook

6 Color the equals sign when it is true.

✕ Cross it out if it is false.

$$4 \boxed{=} 3 \qquad\qquad 12 + 0 \boxed{=} 10 + 2$$

$$5 + 6 \boxed{=} 12 \qquad\qquad 10 + 10 \boxed{=} 18 + 1$$

$$5 \boxed{=} 5 \qquad\qquad 11 + 4 \boxed{=} 15$$

 $\boxed{=}$  $\boxed{=}$

  $\boxed{=}$

7 Make these equal sums true.

$$10 + 1 = 9 + \boxed{} \qquad 12 + 4 = \boxed{} + 3$$

$$10 + \boxed{} = 12 + 1 \qquad 15 + \boxed{} = 16 + 2$$

$$\boxed{} + 4 = 13 + 1 \qquad 5 + 5 = \boxed{} + \boxed{}$$

I finished this lesson online.	This pet hatched.	I can	Driving tests
	**Layla the** ___	• Use the equals sign to show that 2 sums are equal ☐	Tick when complete. Operations 10, 11: Addition sums ☐ Subtraction sums ☐

1 ✏️ Complete the number lines.

Count by 2s.

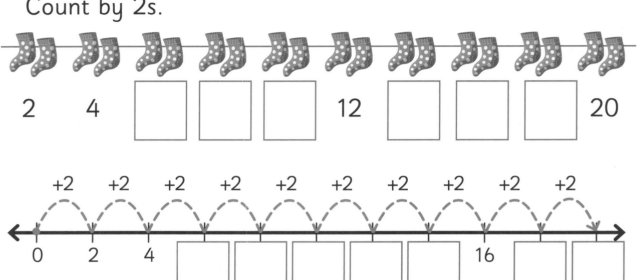

2   4   ☐   ☐   ☐   12   ☐   ☐   ☐   20

Count by 5s.

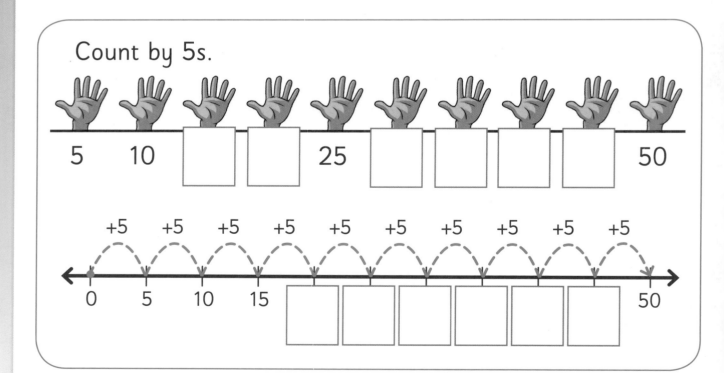

5   10   ☐   ☐   25   ☐   ☐   ☐   ☐   50

Counting by 2s and 5s

② ✏️ Draw 2 cookies in each jar.

Count by 2s. How many cookies? ☐

③ ✏️ Draw 5 eggs in each nest.

Count by 5s. How many eggs? ☐

④ ✏️ Make jumps of 2. Write the number you land on.

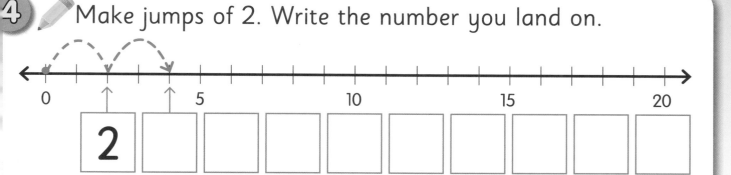

5 (Circle) groups of 2.

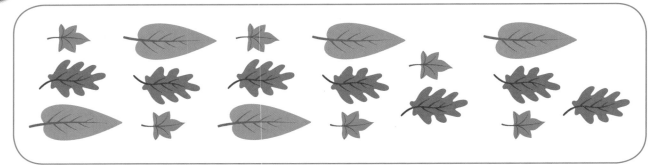

How many groups?

How many leaves altogether? ☐

6 (Circle) groups of 5.

How many groups?

How many beans altogether?

7 ✏ Skip count to add.

   **+**   **=**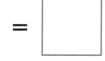

Mathseeds First Grade Workbook

Counting by 2s and 5s

8 ✏️ Write the answers.

2 + 2 = ☐

2 groups of 2 = ☐

2 + 2 + 2 = ☐

3 groups of 2 = ☐

2 + 2 + 2 + 2 = ☐

4 groups of 2 = ☐

2 + 2 + 2 + 2 + 2 = ☐

5 groups of 2 = ☐

7 groups of 2 = ☐

8 groups of 2 = ☐

9 How many eyes on:

1 starfish? ☐

5 starfish? ☐

8 starfish? ☐

10 How many legs on:

3 starfish? ☐

10 starfish? ☐

1 Put your hands like this. Color the **L**.

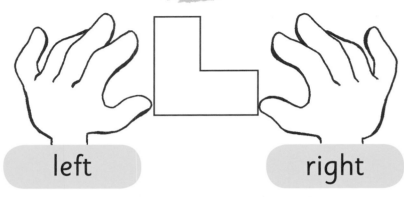

left   right

2 In each pair color **left** yellow, **right** red.

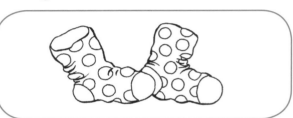
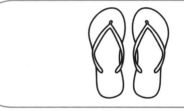
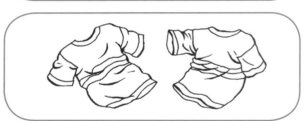

3 Circle the dogs that face **left**. ←

4 Circle the fish that face **right**. →

Mathseeds First Grade Workbook

5 ✏️ Write **left** or **right**.

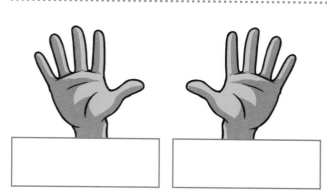

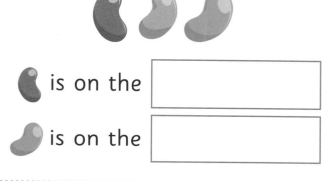

🫘 is on the [＿＿＿＿]

🫘 is on the [＿＿＿＿]

Dizzy is on the [＿＿＿＿]

Mango is on the [＿＿＿＿]

6 Color

the **left** one **blue**.
the **right** one **pink**.
the **middle** one **orange**.

7

✏️ Draw a ● to the **right**.
Draw a ● to the **left**.

8 ✏️ Draw

· a flower 🌸 to the **right** of the tree.

· a bird 🐦 **above** the tree.

· an apple 🍎 **under** the tree.

· a ball ⚽ to the **left** of the tree.

9 Go left 1 ←, up 2 ↑, right 3 →, down 2 ↓, right 1 →, up 3 ↑, left 1 ←.

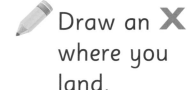 Draw an **X** where you land.

	START			

10 Follow directions to find the treasure.

- Start here
- up 2
- left 3
- up 1
- right 2
- up 1
- right 2   Now draw the treasure in this square!

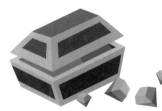

I finished this lesson online.	This pet hatched.	I can	Driving tests
78	Samara the	• Identify left and right ☐ • Follow directions ☐	Tick when complete. Geometry 4, 5: Above and below ☐ Left and right ☐

1 Match.

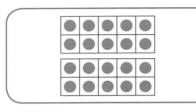

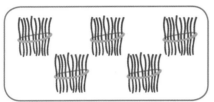

tens	ones
8	0

seventy

10
20
30
40
50
60
70
80
90
100

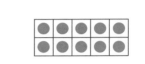

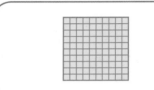

sixty

tens	ones
9	0

2 Match.

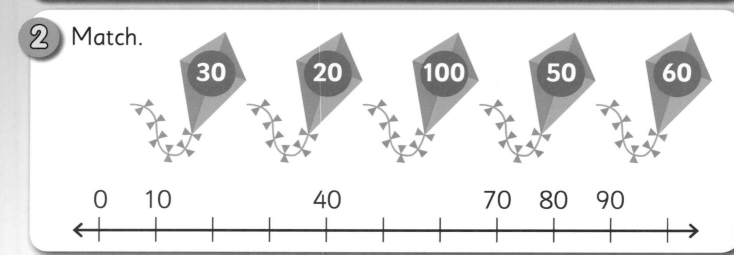

30   20   100   50   60

0   10   40   70   80   90

3 (Circle) groups of ten.

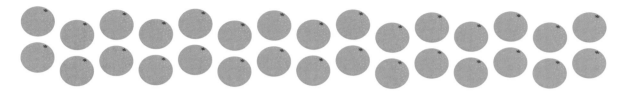

Count by 10s. How many altogether? ☐

Count by 10s. How many altogether? ☐

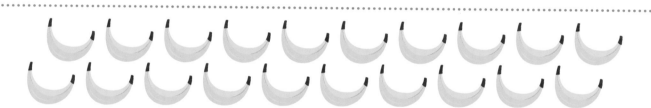

Count by 10s. How many altogether? ☐

4 Order the numbers. Write in the bubbles.

○ ○ ○   ○ ○ ○

30 **10** **20**   **60** **40** **50**

○ ○ ○ ○

90 **80** **100** **70**

5 ✂ Cut out the groups of numbers on page 255. Paste them in the correct place on the chart.

1	2	3	4	5					
11	12	13	14	15	16	17			
21	22	23	24	25	26	27	28	29	30
		33	34	35	36	37	38		
					46	47	48		
51	52	53	54	55	56	57	58		
61	62	63	64	65	66	67	68	69	70
	72	73	74	75	76	77			80
				85	86	87			
				95	96	97			

6 Color the 10s pattern.

7 ✏ What is the same in all the tens?

_____

8 How do the tens change?

_____

Mathseeds First Grade Workbook

Counting by 10s

9 Complete the number line.

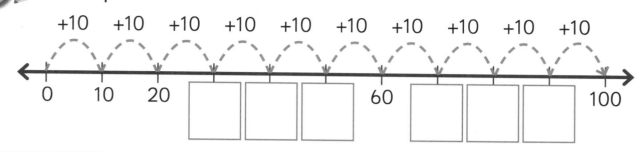

+10 +10 +10 +10 +10 +10 +10 +10 +10 +10

0   10   20   [ ]   [ ]   [ ]   60   [ ]   [ ]   [ ]   100

10 Count by 10s. Circle the odd number out.

10   20   30   31   40   50

80   70   60   50   40   35

30   40   50   56   60   70

100   90   80   70   63   60

11 Write 10 more than each number.

| 8 | 12 | 27 | 39 |

Mathseeds First Grade Workbook

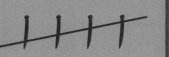

1 Dizzy collected eggs. He made this table.

(eggs)	3
(eggs)	4
(eggs)	2

How many  ? ☐   How many ? ☐

How many ? ☐   How many altogether? ☐

Which egg is there most of? ⬭

Which egg is there least of? ⬭

2 Count. ✏ Write the totals.

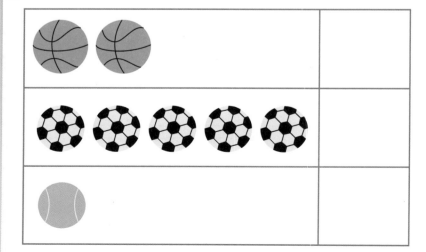

What could this table show?

_____

_____

_____

_____

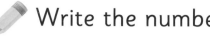
③ Count the tally marks. ✏️ Write the number.

$$\cancel{||||} = 5$$

⭐	I I I I	
⭐	$\cancel{||||}$ I I I	
⭐	$\cancel{||||}$ I	

Which is there most of?

Which is there least of?

How many starfish altogether?

④ ✏️ Write these numbers in tally marks.

1	7
5	10
3	9

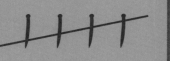

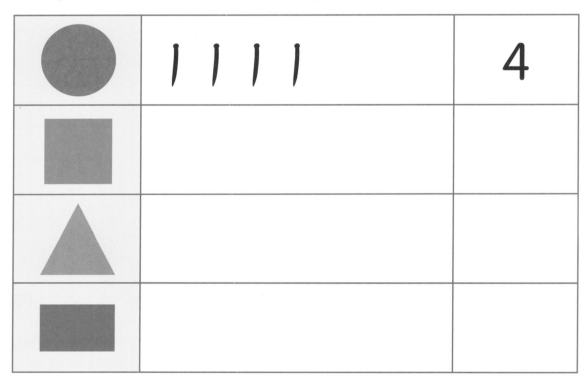

5 Complete the table. Use tally marks, then numbers.

●	l l l l	4
■		
▲		
▬		

6 Which shape is there most of?

7 Which shape is there least of?

8 How many shapes are there altogether?

Mathseeds First Grade Workbook

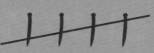

9 This is a graph of the Chu family's fruit today.

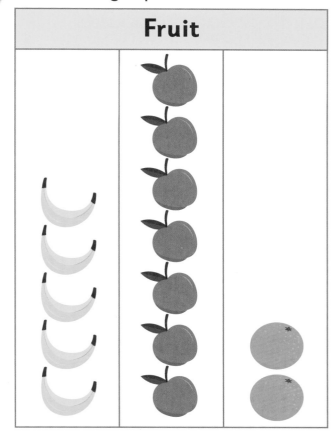

How many ? ☐

How many 🍎? ☐

How many 🍊? ☐

How many pieces of fruit altogether? ☐

What is the most popular fruit? _____

What is the least popular fruit? _____

10 Change this graph into a tally table.

I finished this lesson online.

80

This pet hatched.

Pearl the _____

I can
- Read data ☐
- Use tally marks ☐
- Complete picture graphs ☐

Driving tests
Tick when complete.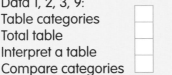
Data 1, 2, 3, 9:
Table categories ☐
Total table ☐
Interpret a table ☐
Compare categories ☐

1 ✏️ Write three sums which equal the same amount.

☐ + ☐ = 10   ☐ + ☐ = 10   ☐ + ☐ = 10

☐ + ☐ = 15   ☐ + ☐ = 15   ☐ + ☐ = 15

☐ + ☐ = 20   ☐ + ☐ = 20   ☐ + ☐ = 20

2 How many

fingers?

 ☐

ears?

 ☐

3 Color 90.

90

Mathseeds First Grade Workbook

4 (Circle)

the left one.	the right one.

5 Complete. Use tally marks, then numbers.

6 Which animal is there most of?

7 Which animal is there least of?

8 How many animals?

Terrific!

YOU COMPLETED

MAP 16

YOU CAN:

☐ Use the **equals sign** to show that two sums are equal.

☐ Skip count by **2s**, **5s**, and **10s**.

☐ Recognize **left** and **right**.

☐ Use **tally marks** and answer questions about **data**.

Signed:

_____

Dated:

Mathseeds First Grade Workbook

Color

the left shoe **blue**.

the right shoe yellow.

the right arm **green**.

the left arm **red**.

the left leg pink.

the right leg **purple**.

the rest of the clown orange.

1 ✏️ Use Ruby's numbers to complete the chart.

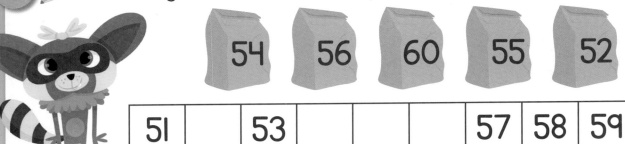

| 54 | 56 | 60 | 55 | 52 |

| 51 | | 53 | | | 57 | 58 | 59 | |

2 ✏️ Match.

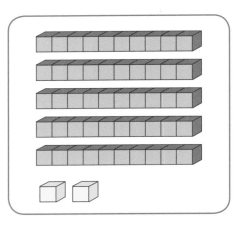

52

54

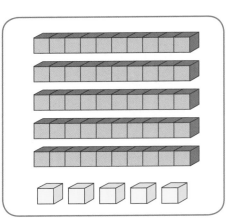

55

fifty-nine

57

sixty

59

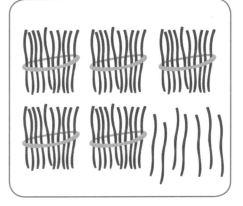

60

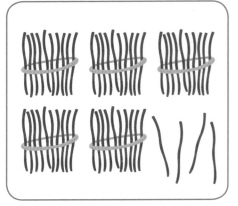

Mathseeds First Grade Workbook

③ ✏️ Complete the number line.

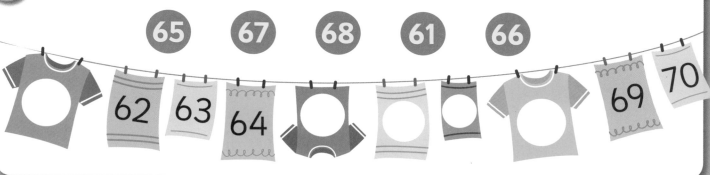

65 67 68 61 66

62 63 64 69 70

④ How many?

70 63 68 62

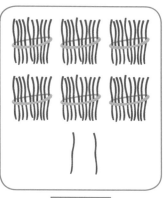 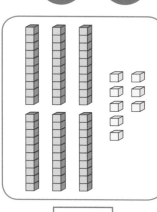 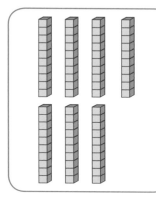 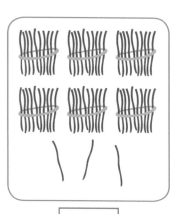

⑤ ✏️ Match.

fifty-six

fifty-nine

fifty-four

68
54
56
62
65
59

sixty-two

sixty-five

sixty-eight

6 Order the numbers. Write them in the snakes.

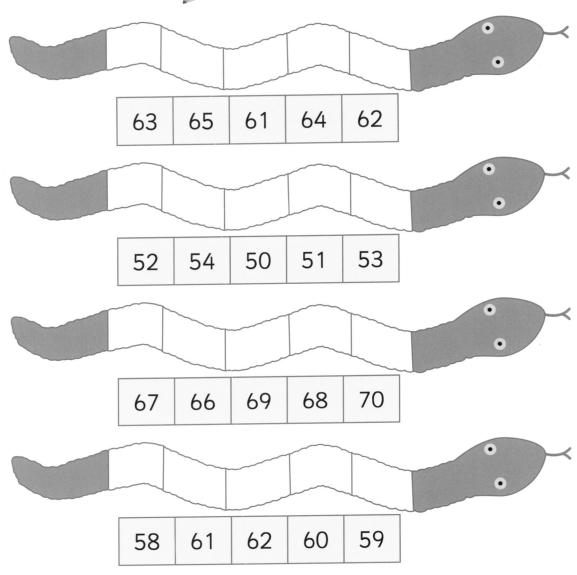

| 63 | 65 | 61 | 64 | 62 |

| 52 | 54 | 50 | 51 | 53 |

| 67 | 66 | 69 | 68 | 70 |

| 58 | 61 | 62 | 60 | 59 |

7 Write the number before.

51 ___   70 ___   68 ___

63 ___   66 ___   52 ___

8 ✏️ Write the number
two more than.

59 _____   **57** _____   **50** _____

two less than.

64 _____   **55** _____   **70** _____

9 (Circle) the biggest number.
Put a cross ✗ on the smallest number.

64 69 60

52 50 56 65

10 ✏️ Write these numbers from smallest to largest.

59 70 65 50 68 53 61 56

_____

I finished this lesson online.	This pet hatched.	I can	Driving tests
(81)	Bruce the	• Recognize and order numbers 50 to 70 ☐	Tick when complete. Number 12: Numbers to 70 ☐

 Mathseeds First Grade Workbook

153

1 ✏️ Write **will**, **won't**, or **might** happen for each picture. Color.

2 (Circle) the picture which is **less likely**.

Color the picture which is **more likely**.

③ 🖊 Draw something that

will happen.	**won't happen.**	**might happen.**

④ Color the correct answer.

When is it more
likely to snow?

(summer) (winter)

Where are you
less likely to
catch a fish?

(sea) (mall)

Where are you more
likely to see cars?

(roads) (space)

When are you less likely
to eat breakfast?

(morning) (night)

Mathseeds First Grade Workbook

5 Color the **possible** animals and ✕ cross out the **impossible** animals.

6 ✏️ Draw a **possible** animal.

7 ✏️ Draw an **impossible** animal.

I finished this lesson online.

This pet hatched.

Yves the

I can
- Recognize that some things are more likely to happen than others ☐

Driving tests
Tick when complete.
Data 5, 7, 11:
Will or won't? ☐☐☐
Might ☐☐☐
Chance

1 Match.

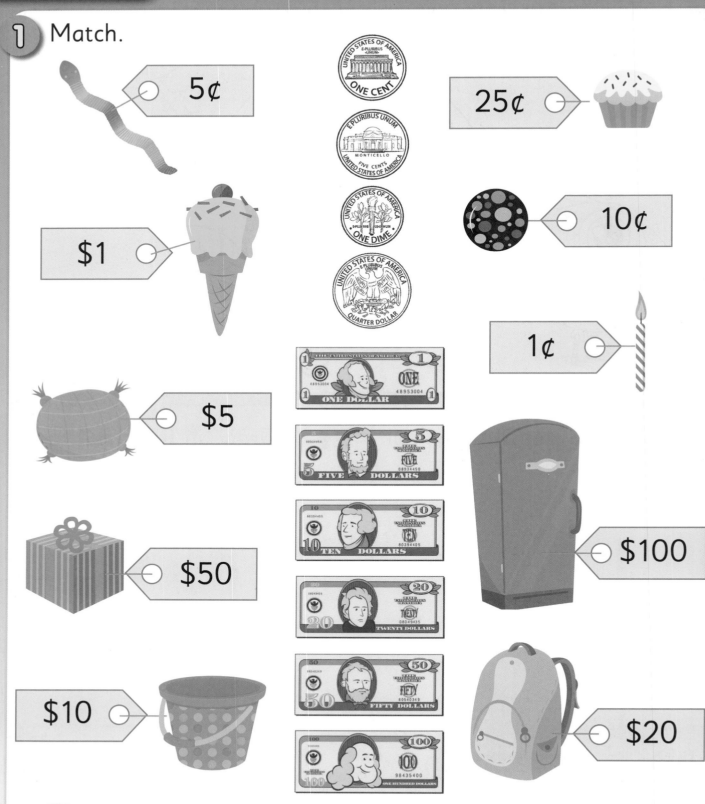

Circle the least expensive item, cross out ✗ the most expensive.

LESSON 83 MONEY · PART 2

② Color the correct amount of money.

$10

$15

$20

$5.50

$2.25

$12.75

 First Grade Workbook

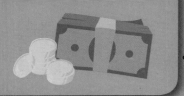
③ (Circle) the most expensive toy, cross out ✕ the cheapest toy.

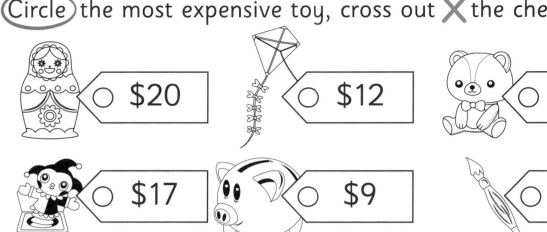

○ $20   ○ $12   ○ $5

○ $17   ○ $9   ○ $1

Color the 3 toys that cost $18 altogether.

④ How much altogether? ✏ Write the total.

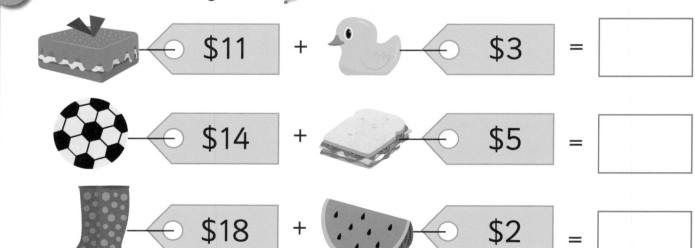

$11 + $3 =

$14 + $5 =

$18 + $2 =

$15 + $1 =

$12 + $7 =

5 Doc buys a bow tie for $8. He buys a hat for $5. How much does he spend altogether?

 Use the number line.

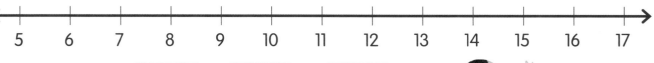

5   6   7   8   9   10   11   12   13   14   15   16   17

Complete. ☐ + ☐ = ☐

Doc spends $ ☐ altogether.

6 Ruby buys a rug for $10, a book for $4, and a bag for $6. How much does she spend altogether?

 Use the number line.

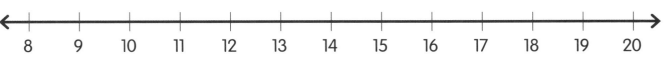

8   9   10   11   12   13   14   15   16   17   18   19   20

Complete. ☐ + ☐ + ☐ = ☐

Ruby spends $ ☐ altogether.

I finished this lesson online.	This pet hatched.	I can	Driving tests
	Gretzky the ___	• Recognize coins and bills ☐ • Add amounts of money to find totals ☐	Tick when complete. Measurement 12: Ordering coins ☐

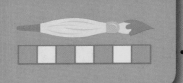
1 Color the longer animal **red** and the shorter animal **blue**.

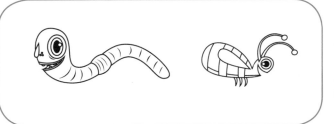

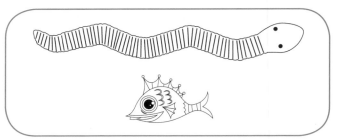

2 Circle the longest. Cross out ✗ the shortest.

3 🖍 Draw

a shorter rocket.

a longer truck.

Mathseeds First Grade Workbook

4 ✂ Cut out the shapes on page 257.
Paste them in order from shortest to longest.

shortest

↓

longest

5 ✂ Cut out the blocks on page 257. Use the blocks to measure the length of each object.

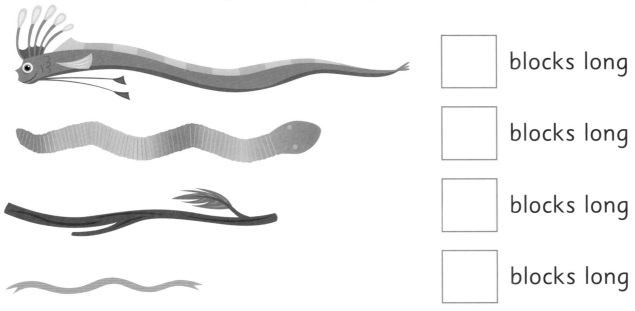

☐ blocks long

☐ blocks long

☐ blocks long

☐ blocks long

Circle the longest object.

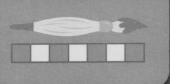

6 How long? Count the blocks.

The pencil is

☐ blocks long.

The sharpener is

☐ blocks long.

The cylinder is

☐ blocks long.

The paintbrush is

☐ blocks long.

The glue stick is

☐ blocks long.

The leaf is

☐ blocks long.

7 Count the lengths. Label them **longer** and **shorter**.

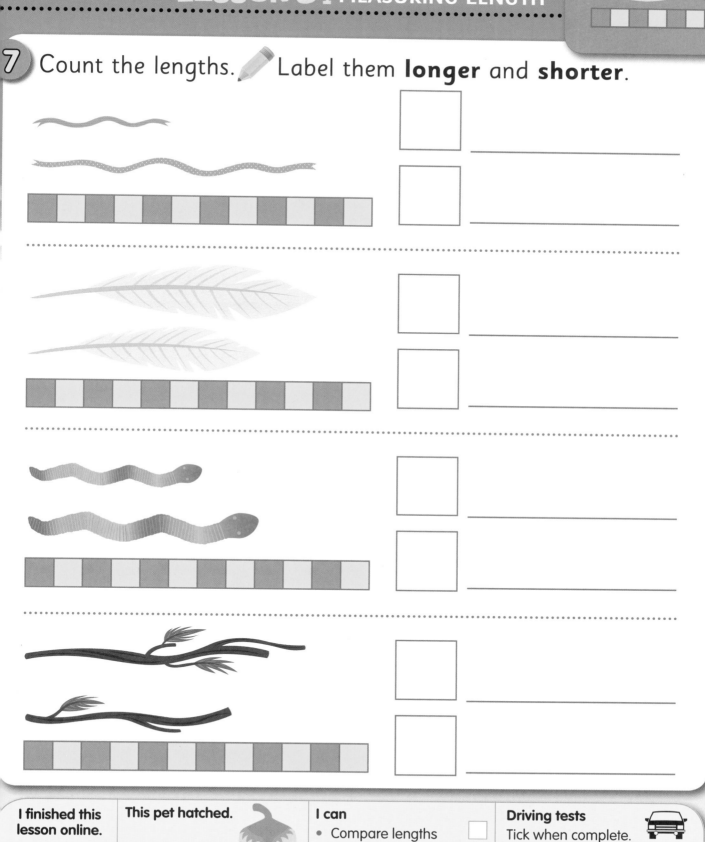

I finished this lesson online.

84

This pet hatched.

Puck the

I can
- Compare lengths
- Measure lengths using blocks

Driving tests
Tick when complete.
Measurement 4, 13, 14:
Comparing lengths
Measuring lengths
How to measure

1 ✏️ What is the difference?

The difference between 17 and 12 is ☐.

2 Find the difference.

20 − 13 = ☐

15 − 7 = ☐

3 Count the spaces. ✏️ Write the answer.

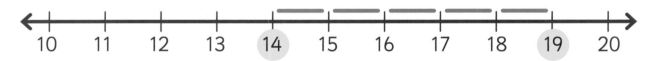

The difference between 19 and 14 is ☐.

④ Count the spaces to find the difference.

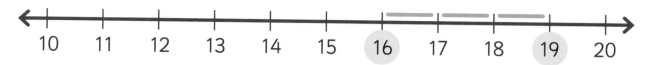

$$19 - 16 = \boxed{}$$

$$16 - 11 = \boxed{}$$

$$20 - 14 = \boxed{}$$

$$18 - 16 = \boxed{}$$

$$17 - 13 = \boxed{}$$

5 Find the difference.

$$18 - 15 = \boxed{}$$

6 Use the number line to find the difference. Complete the sum.

Mango has 17 apples. Ruby has 8 pears.
What is the difference?

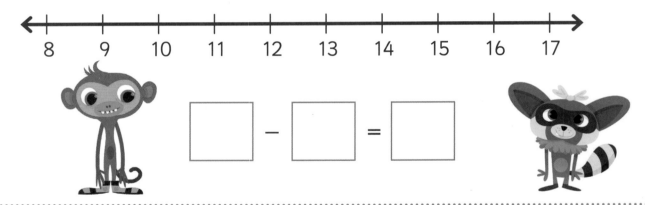

$$\boxed{} - \boxed{} = \boxed{}$$

Waldo has 19 carrots. Doc has 15 beans.
What is the difference?

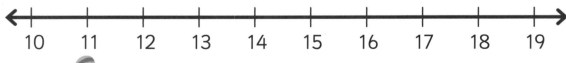

 $\boxed{} - \boxed{} = \boxed{}$

Mathseeds First Grade Workbook

7 What is the difference between 15 books and 9 books.

 Draw a picture.

Use the number line.

8   9   10   11   12   13   14   15   16   17   18

Complete the sentence.

The difference between and is .

Complete the sum.

☐ — ☐ = ☐

THE SEVEN SILLY SHEEP

I finished this lesson online.

85

This pet hatched.

Rob the

I can

• Find the difference between two numbers on a number line ☐

Mathseeds First Grade Workbook

169

1 Complete the number lines.

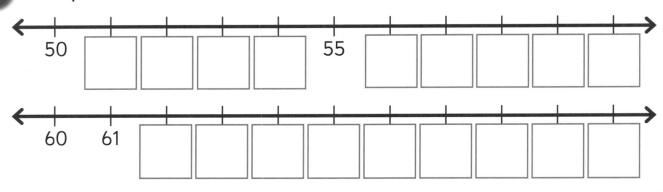

50 [ ] [ ] [ ] [ ] 55 [ ] [ ] [ ] [ ] [ ]

60 61 [ ] [ ] [ ] [ ] [ ] [ ] [ ] [ ]

2 ✏️ Draw something that

will happen.	won't happen.

3 How many beads long is each line?

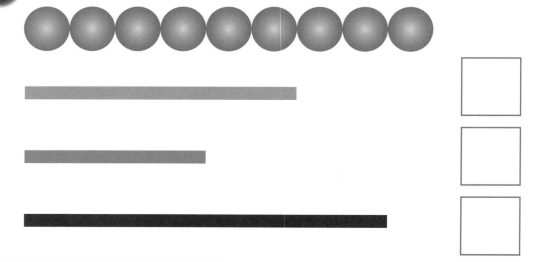

[ ]

[ ]

[ ]

4 Color the money to make the amount.

35¢

$1.50

$20

5 Complete.

The difference between ⬜ and ⬜ is ⬜ .

6 Count the spaces to find the difference.

$$20 - 13 = \boxed{}$$

Yippee!

YOU COMPLETED

MAP 17

YOU CAN:

- [ ] Order numbers **50** to **70**.
- [ ] Identify events that **will** and **won't** happen.
- [ ] Measure **lengths**.
- [ ] Match amounts to the correct **coins** and **bills**.
- [ ] **Find the difference** between two numbers to 20.

Signed:

_____

Dated:

Mathseeds First Grade Workbook

1 Help everyone find the matching amount of money.

$16 $2.50 $21.25   20¢

1 ✏️ Match.

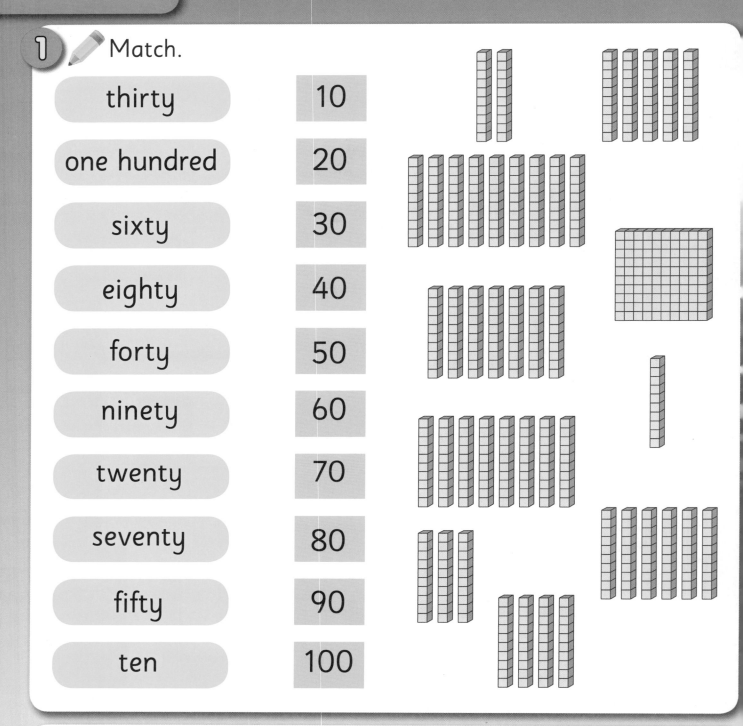

thirty	10
one hundred	20
sixty	30
eighty	40
forty	50
ninety	60
twenty	70
seventy	80
fifty	90
ten	100

2 ✏️ Complete.

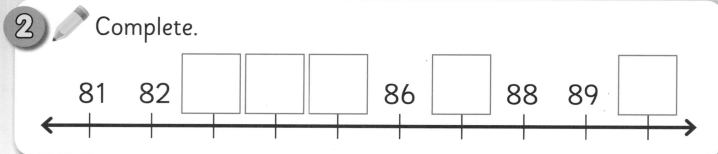

81 82 ☐ ☐ ☐ 86 ☐ 88 89 ☐

Counting 70 to 100

3 Complete the number chart.

61	62	63				67	68	69	
			74	75	76				80
81					86	87	88		
		93			96	97			

4 Join the snakes together to make number lines.

 81 82 83 84

90 91 92

 94 95 96 97

76 77 78

 72 73 74 75

85 86 87

 86 87 88 89

98 99 100

5 Write the missing numbers.

 90 ◯ **92**

62 **63** ◯

◯ **80** ◯

69 ◯ **71**

6 ✏️ Write the number before.

80		72		91	
100		78		97	

7 How many?

 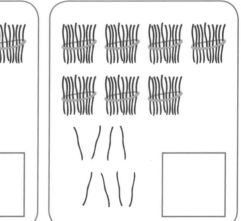

8 Make **61** ★.

9 Make **76** ▲.

Mathseeds First Grade Workbook

10 (Circle) the biggest number.
Put a cross ✗ on the smallest number.

 78 87 80   78 87 80

 70 100 79

11 ✏️ Write in order, **smallest** to **largest**.

56 100 73 | 93 79 48

☐ ☐ ☐   ☐ ☐ ☐

12 ✏️ Write each number in the correct box.

72 19 37
80 3 46
12 68 24

 Under 20    20 to 50    50 to 100

I finished this lesson online. (86)

This pet hatched. Tong the _____

I can
• Recognize and order numbers 70 to 100 ☐

Driving tests
Tick when complete. 🚗
Number 13, 15, 16:
Order to 120 ☐
Before and after ☐
Sequence to 120 ☐

Mathseeds First Grade Workbook   177

1 🖊 Write the minutes on the digital clocks.

half-past 4
four-thirty

half-past 8
eight-thirty

half-past 5
five-thirty

half-past 11
eleven-thirty

half-past 1
one-thirty

half-past 7
seven-thirty

2 Match.

half-past 6

three-thirty

half-past 2

half-past 12

half-past 9

ten-thirty

③ What time is it?   **11**   **ten**   **one**   **4**

half-past _____

_____ thirty

half-past _____

half-past _____

④ 🖉 Trace the lines to find the matching times.
Write each time.

half-past _____   half-past _____   half-past _____

5 Match.

6 Write the digital times on the clocks.

ten-thirty
half-past 10

four-thirty
half-past 4

two-thirty
half-past 2

7 Draw something you might do at **6:30** in the evening.

(8) What is the time one hour later?

two-thirty + 1 hour =

seven-thirty + 1 hour =

twelve-thirty + 1 hour =

five-thirty + 1 hour =

nine-thirty + 1 hour =

four-thirty + 1 hour =

| I finished this lesson online.  | This pet hatched.  Manda the | I can • Read and write half hour times on digital clocks ☐ • Add one hour to a time ☐ | Driving tests 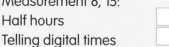 Tick when complete. Measurement 8, 15: Half hours ☐ Telling digital times ☐ |

Mathseeds First Grade Workbook

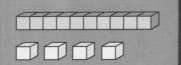

1 Count how many. Match to a number.

14

16

18

7

9

20

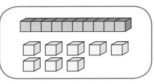

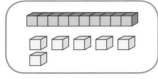

2 Write the number. How many tens and ones?

fourteen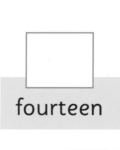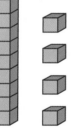

[ ] tens [ ] ones

sixteen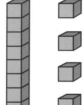

[ ] tens [ ] ones

fifteen

[ ] tens [ ] ones

thirteen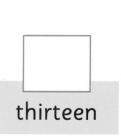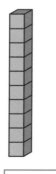

[ ] tens [ ] ones

Mathseeds First Grade Workbook

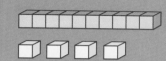

3 Match.

Tens	Ones
1	8

Tens	Ones
2	0

10 + 5

10 + 10

10 + 8

10 + 6

Tens	Ones
1	5

Tens	Ones
1	6

4 Trade 10 ones for a ten. What is the number?
The first is done for you.

Tens	Ones	
		12

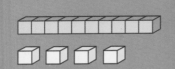

5 Trade 10 ones for another ten. What is the number?

Tens	Ones	

6 Add 4 more ones. Trade for a ten. Find the answer.

Tens	Ones	
		29 + 4 =
		17 + 4 =
		36 + 4 =
		26 + 4 =

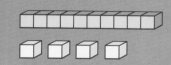

7 Find the answer. Show your working.

Mango has 9 balls and finds 7 more.

How many altogether? ☐

Ruby buys 15 carrots and 6 potatoes.

How many altogether? ☐

Dizzy ate 28 cherries and 4 pears.

How many altogether? ☐

Waldo sees 33 birds and 8 fish.

How many altogether? ☐

I finished this lesson online.	This pet hatched.	I can	Driving tests
⊙88⊙	Li the ☐	• Trade ten ones blocks for a ten stick ☐ • Trade ones for tens when adding ☐	Tick when complete. Number 9, 10: Place value to 50 ☐ Partitioning to 50 ☐

1 ✏️ Order the containers from **largest** to **smallest** capacity by numbering them from 1 to 4.

2 Circle the best thing to use to fill each item.

3 Ruby used a mug to fill each item.

 4  6  7

✓ the one that holds the most.

✗ the one that holds the least

4 ✏️ Estimate how many times you would use the container to fill each item.

 = ☐

 = ☐

 = ☐

 = ☐

 = ☐

 = ☐

5 Gather these containers and a cup.

Container	Estimate	Measure	Difference
vase			
ice cream container			
cake tin			
water bottle			
small juice bottle			

6 Estimate how many cups of water each container will hold.

7 Use the cup to fill them with water. How many cups do they hold?

8 ✓ the ones you got right.

✏ Write the difference for the others.

9 Color the best container for holding

ice cream.

clothes.

money.

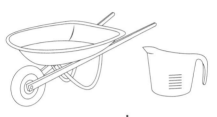

sand.

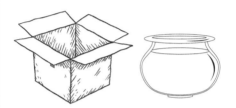

toys.

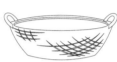

school books.

10 Match.

I finished this lesson online.	This pet hatched.	I can	Driving tests
 89	Katy the	• Measure capacity using smaller containers • Compare capacity of containers	Tick when complete. 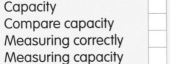 Measurement 11, 17, 18, 19: Capacity Compare capacity Measuring correctly Measuring capacity

1 ✏️ Complete the skip counting number lines.

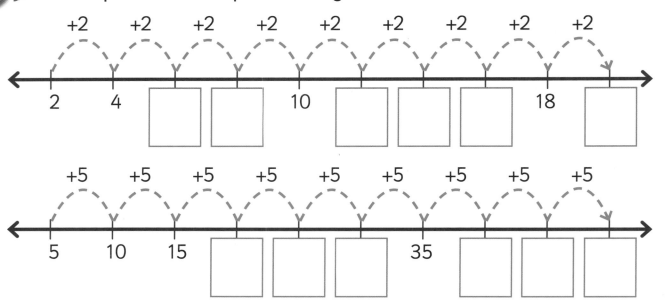

+2 +2 +2 +2 +2 +2 +2 +2 +2

2 4 ☐ ☐ 10 ☐ ☐ ☐ 18 ☐

+5 +5 +5 +5 +5 +5 +5 +5 +5

5 10 15 ☐ ☐ ☐ 35 ☐ ☐ ☐

2 ✏️ Write the missing numbers.

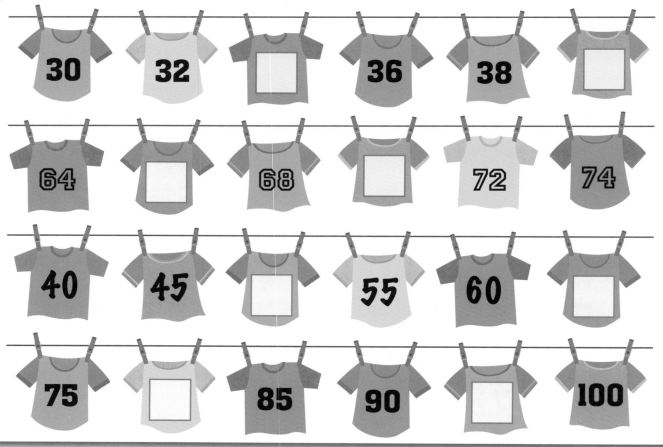

30 32 ☐ 36 38 ☐

64 ☐ 68 ☐ 72 74

40 45 ☐ 55 60 ☐

75 ☐ 85 90 ☐ 100

Mathseeds First Grade Workbook

1 2 3 4 5 6 7 8 9 10

③ Count by 2s and color the squares **blue**.

④ Count by 5s and color the squares **red**.

1	2	3	4	5	6	7	8	9	10
11	12	13	14	15	16	17	18	19	20
21	22	23	24	25	26	27	28	29	30
31	32	33	34	35	36	37	38	39	40
41	42	43	44	45	46	47	48	49	50
51	52	53	54	55	56	57	58	59	60
61	62	63	64	65	66	67	68	69	70
71	72	73	74	75	76	77	78	79	80
81	82	83	84	85	86	87	88	89	90
91	92	93	94	95	96	97	98	99	100

⑤ What do the count by 5s end with? ☐ and ☐

⑥ What do the count by 2s end with? ☐ ☐ ☐

☐ and ☐

⑦ Circle the numbers that you can count by 5s and also count by 2s.

8 ✂ Cut out the nickels on page 257.
Paste them to show the correct amount.

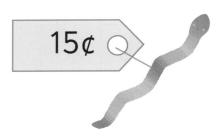

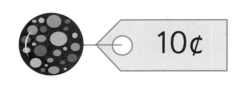

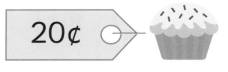

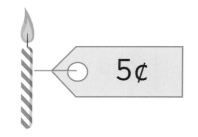

⑨ 🖉 Use skip counting to find the answer. Show your working.

Dizzy has 5 tanks. There are 2 crabs in each tank.
How many crabs altogether?

☐ crabs altogether

Waldo has 6 bowls. There are 5 fish in each bowl.
How many fish altogether?

☐ fish altogether

Mango has 9 boxes. There are 2 shoes in each box.
How many shoes altogether?

☐ shoes altogether

I finished this lesson online.	This pet hatched.	I can	Driving tests
⑨⓪	Zhao the ☐	• Skip count by 2s and 5s ☐ • Use skip counting to solve word problems ☐	Tick when complete. Patterns and Fractions 10, 12: Counting patterns ☐ Place value patterns ☐

Mathseeds First Grade Workbook

193

1 ✏️ Complete.

Clock time	Digital time	One hour later
(clock showing 3:30)		
(clock showing 9:30)		

2 ✏️ Complete the number lines.

71 ☐ ☐ ☐ 75 ☐ ☐ ☐ 79 ☐

☐ ☐ 83 ☐ ☐ ☐ 87 ☐ ☐ ☐

☐ 92 ☐ ☐ ☐ ☐ ☐ ☐ ☐

3 ✏️ Order the containers from **smallest** to **largest** capacity. Number them 1 to 4.

 ☐ ☐  ☐ ☐

4 ✏️ Write the numbers.

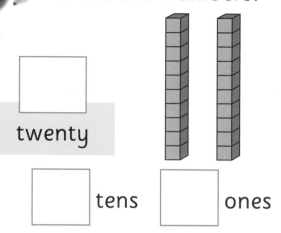

twenty

[ ] tens [ ] ones

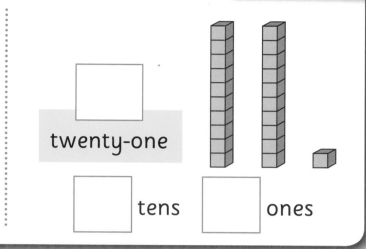

twenty-one

[ ] tens [ ] ones

5 ✏️ What is the next number?

20 22 24 26 [ ]

52 54 56 58 [ ]

76 78 80 82 [ ]

92 94 96 98 [ ]

15 20 25 30 [ ]

45 50 55 60 [ ]

60 65 70 75 [ ]

80 85 90 95 [ ]

6 Add 6 more ones. Trade 10 ones for a ten. Find the answer.

Tens	Ones	
	▱ ▱ ▱ ▱ ▱ ▱ ▱ ▱ ▱	19 + 6 = [ ]
	▱ ▱ ▱ ▱ ▱	35 + 6 = [ ]

Amazing!

YOU COMPLETED

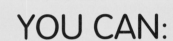

MAP 18

YOU CAN:

- [ ] Read and write **digital half-hour times**.
- [ ] **Add one hour** to digital times.
- [ ] Count numbers **70** to **100**.
- [ ] Order the **capacity** of containers.
- [ ] **Trade** ten ones for one ten stick when adding.

Signed:

_____

Dated:

Mathseeds First Grade Workbook

1 Find the number. Color the matching square on the chart.

◼ = |||| ▫

◻ = (ten frame with 8 dots)

◼ = |||||| ▫▫▫

◻ = twenty

◼ = (hundred grid)

◼ = forty

◻ = (tally marks)

◼ = eighty-two

◼ =
tens	ones
7	4

1	2	3	4	5	6	7	8	9	10
11	12	13	14	15	16	17	18	19	20
21	22	23	24	25	26	27	28	29	30
31	32	33	34	35	36	37	38	39	40
41	42	43	44	45	46	47	48	49	50
51	52	53	54	55	56	57	58	59	60
61	62	63	64	65	66	67	68	69	70
71	72	73	74	75	76	77	78	79	80
81	82	83	84	85	86	87	88	89	90
91	92	93	94	95	96	97	98	99	100

1 Color the near doubles dominoes.

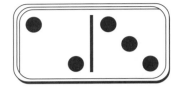  

2 Complete.

2 + 3 = ?

THINK double 2 plus 1

2 + 2 = ☐   plus 1 = ☐

2 + 3 = ☐

---

5 + 6 = ?

THINK double 5 plus 1

5 + 5 = ☐   plus 1 = ☐

5 + 6 = ☐

---

4 + 6 = ?

THINK double 4 plus 2

4 + 4 = ☐   plus 2 = ☐

4 + 6 = ☐

6 + 8 = ?

THINK double 6 plus 2

6 + 6 = ☐   plus 2 = ☐

6 + 8 = ☐

③ ✏️ Match each sum to its nearest double.

9 + 10 =   4 + 5 =   1 + 2 =   6 + 7 =

(10 + 10)   (1 + 1)   (9 + 9)   (4 + 4)

(5 + 5)   (3 + 3)   (7 + 7)   (6 + 6)

10 + 11 =   5 + 6 =   3 + 4 =   7 + 8 =

④ ✏️ Match each bone to the correct dog.

 17

8 + 8 = 16
16 + **1** = 17

(6 + 8 =)

 (3 + 5 =)

 8

3 + 3 = 6
6 + **2** = 8

 14

6 + 6 = 12
12 + **2** = 14

(8 + 9 =)

(7 + 8 =)

 15

7 + 7 = 14
14 + **1** = 15

⑤ ✏️ Complete.

7 + 8   = 7 + 7 + 1   = ☐

5 + 6   = 5 + 5 + 1   = ☐

 ✏️ Add Ruby's near double dice rolls.

  ☐ + ☐ + 1 = ☐

  ☐ + ☐ + 1 = ☐

  ☐ + ☐ + 1 = ☐

  ☐ + ☐ + 1 = ☐

  ☐ + ☐ + 1 = ☐

  ☐ + ☐ + 1 = ☐

  ☐ + ☐ + 1 = ☐

  ☐ + ☐ + 1 = ☐

  ☐ + ☐ + 1 = ☐

Mathseeds First Grade Workbook

7 ✏️ Doc has 8 books and Mango has 9 books.
How many books altogether?

Use near doubles.
Show your working.

8 What comes out of the **doubles** machines?

9 What comes out of the **near doubles** machines?

I finished this lesson online.

This pet hatched.

Moira the

I can
• Use near doubles to add ☐
• Double the smaller number
  and add 1 or 2 ☐

Mathseeds First Grade Workbook

1 Count back to find the change.

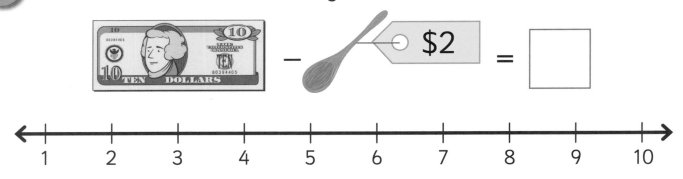

$10 − $2 = ☐

1 2 3 4 5 6 7 8 9 10

$10 − $6 = ☐

1 2 3 4 5 6 7 8 9 10

2 How much change from $10?

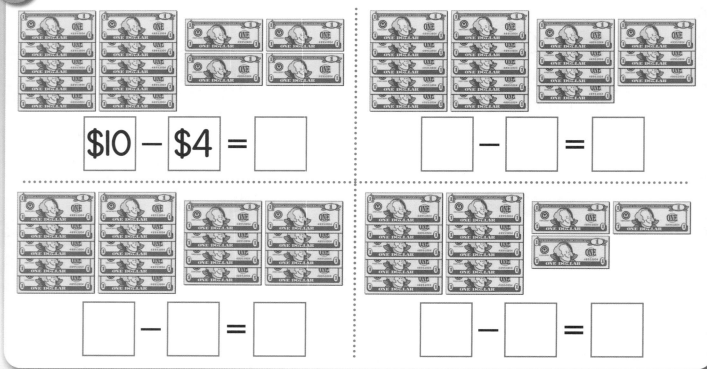

$10 − $4 = ☐

☐ − ☐ = ☐

☐ − ☐ = ☐

☐ − ☐ = ☐

3 Count back to find the change.

 $-$ 🥣 ○ $11 = ☐

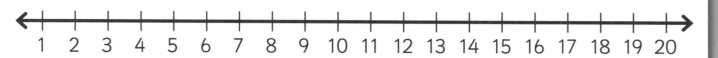

| 1 | 2 | 3 | 4 | 5 | 6 | 7 | 8 | 9 | 10 | 11 | 12 | 13 | 14 | 15 | 16 | 17 | 18 | 19 | 20 |

 $-$ ○ $14 = ☐

| 1 | 2 | 3 | 4 | 5 | 6 | 7 | 8 | 9 | 10 | 11 | 12 | 13 | 14 | 15 | 16 | 17 | 18 | 19 | 20 |

4 Find the change from $20.

 ○ $5

$20 $-$ **$5** = ☐

 ○ $9

$20 $-$ ☐ = ☐

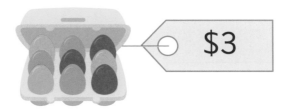 ○ $3

$20 $-$ ☐ = ☐

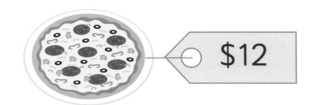 ○ $12

$20 $-$ ☐ = ☐

5 ✂ Cut out the bills on page 259. Paste them to show the correct change for each item. Complete each sum.

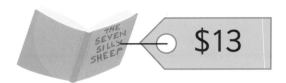

$20 – $13 = ⬜

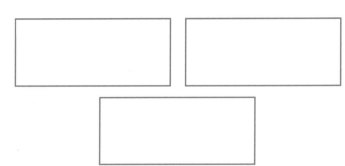

$20 – $15 = ⬜

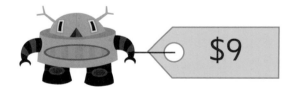

$20 – ⬜ = ⬜

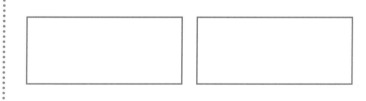

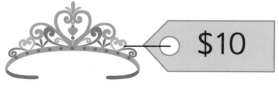

$20 – ⬜ = ⬜

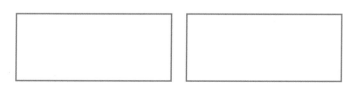

Mathseeds First Grade Workbook

6 Solve the word problems.

Ruby buys a pencil for $1, a ruler for $2, and a note pad for $4.

How much does she spend?

☐ + ☐ + ☐ = ☐

How much change does she get from $10?

☐ − ☐ = ☐

Waldo buys a ball for $3, a jump rope for $4, and a drink bottle for $8.

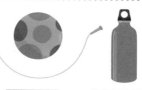

How much does he spend?

☐ + ☐ + ☐ = ☐

How much change does he get from $20?

☐ − ☐ = ☐

Dizzy buys carrots for $2, potatoes for $4, and sausages for $5.

How much does he spend?

☐ + ☐ + ☐ = ☐

How much change does he get from $20?

☐ − ☐ = ☐

I finished this lesson online.

92

This pet hatched.

Leroy the

_____

I can
- Add amounts to find the total ☐
- Subtract to find the change from $10 and $20 ☐

1 ✏️ Write two addition sums for each picture.

$3 + 2 =$ ☐

$2 + 3 =$ ☐

$5 +$ ☐ $=$ ☐

$1 +$ ☐ $=$ ☐

☐ $+$ ☐ $=$ ☐

☐ $+$ ☐ $=$ ☐

☐ $+$ ☐ $=$ ☐

☐ $+$ ☐ $=$ ☐

  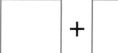 

☐ $+$ ☐ $=$ ☐

☐ $+$ ☐ $=$ ☐

② Complete the related subtraction sums.

$10 - 4 = \boxed{}$ $5 - 1 = \boxed{}$ $8 - 3 = \boxed{}$

$10 - 6 = \boxed{}$ $5 - 4 = \boxed{}$ $8 - 5 = \boxed{}$

$6 - 3 = \boxed{}$ $9 - 2 = \boxed{}$ $7 - 1 = \boxed{}$

$6 - \boxed{} = \boxed{}$ $9 - \boxed{} = \boxed{}$ $7 - \boxed{} = \boxed{}$

③ Draw lines to match the related sums.

$8 - 5 = 3$

$18 - 3 = 15$

$8 + 4 = 12$

$8 - 3 = 5$

$12 - 8 = 4$

$6 - 5 = 1$

$6 - 1 = 5$

$15 + 3 = 18$

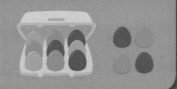

④ ✏ Complete.

☐ + 4 = 9

4 + ☐ = 9

9 − ☐ = 5

☐ − 5 = 4

☐ + 3 = 11

☐ + 8 = 11

☐ − 8 = 3

11 − ☐ = 8

☐ + 7 = 10

☐ + 3 = 10

10 − ☐ = 3

☐ − 3 = 7

5 ✏️ Complete the number fact families.

9 + 8 = ☐

☐ + ☐ = ☐

☐ − ☐ = ☐

☐ − ☐ = ☐

8 + 7 = ☐

☐ + ☐ = ☐

☐ − ☐ = ☐

☐ − ☐ = ☐

6 ✏️ Use each pair of numbers to write a number fact family.

9 and 4

☐ + ☐ = ☐

☐ + ☐ = ☐

☐ − ☐ = ☐

☐ − ☐ = ☐

7 and 5

☐ + ☐ = ☐

☐ + ☐ = ☐

☐ − ☐ = ☐

☐ − ☐ = ☐

7 Roll two dice and use the numbers to write a number fact family. ☐

I finished this lesson online.	This pet hatched.	I can	Driving tests
93	Joshie the ☐	• Use number fact families to complete sums ☐	Tick when complete. Operations 16: Number fact families ☐

🌱 Mathseeds First Grade Workbook

209

1 ✏️ Label the turns **clockwise** or **counterclockwise**.

2 Match.

up

turn left

turn clockwise

turn right

turn counterclockwise

down

3 Color the clockwise turns **red** and the counterclockwise turns **blue**.

Circle the correct answer. What is

above the  ?      

underneath the ?

on top of the  ?   

to the left of the ?

to the right of the ?

in between and ?

5 ✏ Draw
- a star above the snowman.
- a tree to the left of the snowman.
- a flower between the tree and the snowman.
- a spider beneath the flower.
- a bird on top of the tree.

6 Follow the directions.
- Up 2
- Right 3
- Up 2
- Left 2
- Down 3
- Right 1
- Down 1 and draw a ★.

START			

7 ✏️ Write **left** and **right**, **above** and **below**, **up** and **down**, **clockwise** or **counterclockwise**.

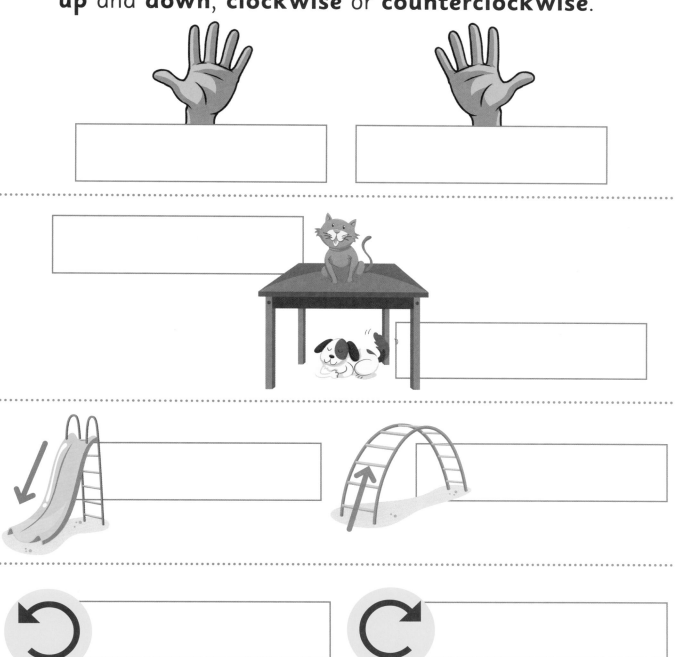

I finished this lesson online.

94

This pet hatched.

Pandora the

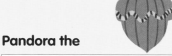

I can
- Recognize clockwise and counterclockwise turns
- Follow directions

Driving tests
Tick when complete.
Geometry 11, 12, 15:
Follow directions
Turns
Giving directions

1 Add.

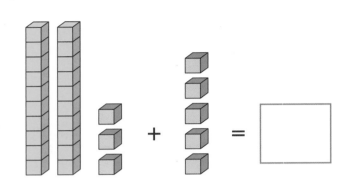 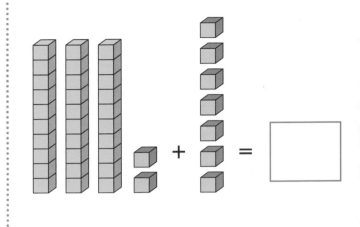

2 ✏️ Draw the tens and ones to add.

43 + 4 = ☐

Tens	Ones

51 + 6 = ☐

Tens	Ones

62 + 5 = ☐

Tens	Ones

76 + 3 = ☐

Tens	Ones

Mathseeds First Grade Workbook

27 + 3 = ☐

③ ✏ Count on to add.

34 + 3 = ☐   37 + 1 = ☐

62 + 6 = ☐   65 + 2 = ☐

④ Count on using the number chart.

43 + 3 = ☐   52 + 3 = ☐   65 + 4 = ☐

54 + 4 = ☐   44 + 2 = ☐   61 + 7 = ☐

44 + 5 = ☐   62 + 4 = ☐   57 + 3 = ☐

41	42	43	44	45	46	47	48	49	50
51	52	53	54	55	56	57	58	59	60
61	62	63	64	65	66	67	68	69	70

5 Use addition strategies to add.

7 + 7 = ☐   8 + 9 = ☐   13 + 4 = ☐

12 + 2 = ☐   34 + 6 = ☐   27 + 3 = ☐

49 + 7 = ☐   55 + 8 = ☐   33 + 9 = ☐

73 + 3 = ☐   66 + 2 = ☐   75 + 3 = ☐

Work space

27 + 3 = ☐

6 Find the answer. Show your working.

Ruby buys 15 ribbons and then 3 more.
How many ribbons altogether? _____

Mango jumps 22 times and then 5 more.
How many jumps altogether? _____

Waldo eats 31 fish and then 8 more.
How many fish altogether? _____

Dizzy has 23 marbles and buys 4 more.
How many marbles altogether? _____

I finished this lesson online.	This pet hatched.	I can	Driving tests
 95	Ethel the	• Use different strategies to add 2 digits to 1 digit ☐	Tick when complete. Operations 10, 15: Add 10 ☐ Add within 10 ☐

1 🖊 Match these near doubles.

11 + 9 =

7 + 6 =

12 + 13 =

13

31

20

25

14

11

8 + 6 =

15 + 16 =

5 + 6 =

2 Match each item to a sum and find the change.

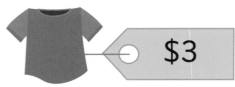 $3

$10 − $3 = ☐

 $7

$10 − $7 = ☐

$18

$20 − $15 = ☐

 $15

$20 − $18 = ☐

3 ✏️ Use each pair of numbers to write a number fact family.

3 and 7

2 and 8

☐ + ☐ = ☐

☐ + ☐ = ☐

☐ − ☐ = ☐

☐ − ☐ = ☐

☐ + ☐ = ☐

☐ + ☐ = ☐

☐ − ☐ = ☐

☐ − ☐ = ☐

4 ✏️ Turn counterclockwise and draw something you see.

5 ✏️ Use addition strategies to add. Show your working.

37 + 8 = ☐

54 + 7 = ☐

Awesome!

YOU COMPLETED

MAP 19

YOU CAN:

- [ ] Use **near doubles** to add.
- [ ] Subtract to find the **change** from $10 and $20.
- [ ] Use **number fact families** to complete sums.
- [ ] Follow **directions**.
- [ ] Use different strategies to **add 2 digits to 1 digit**.

Signed:

_____

Dated:

Mathseeds First Grade Workbook

1 Use the numbers in each egg to complete the sums.

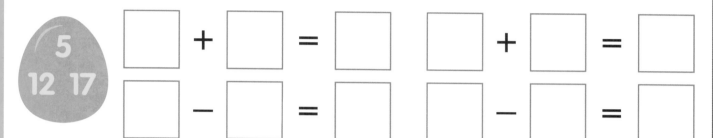

5
12 17

☐ + ☐ = ☐   ☐ + ☐ = ☐

☐ − ☐ = ☐   ☐ − ☐ = ☐

. . . .

3
10 13

☐ + ☐ = ☐   ☐ + ☐ = ☐

☐ − ☐ = ☐   ☐ − ☐ = ☐

2 Crack the code to answer the sums.

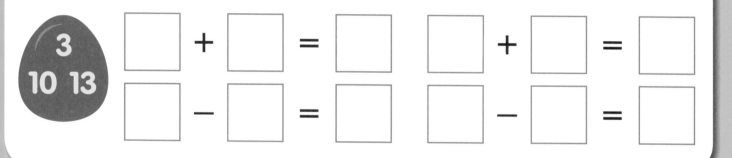

= 1

= 2

= 3

= 4

= 5

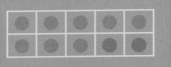

1. Move counters to make 10, then add the leftover counters. The first one is done for you.

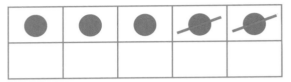

8 + 5 =   10 + 3 = 13

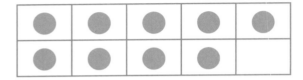

9 + 3 =

10 + ☐ = ☐

7 + 4 =

10 + ☐ = ☐

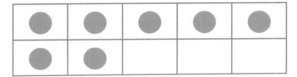

☐ + ☐ =

10 + ☐ = ☐

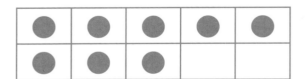 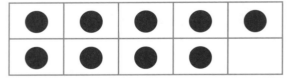

☐ + ☐ =

10 + ☐ = ☐

Mathseeds First Grade Workbook

2 ✏️ Use the number lines to bridge 10. Find the answers.

8 + 9 = ☐

+ 2   + 7

6 7 **8** 9 **10** 11 12 13 14 15 16 17 18 19 20

7 + 5 = ☐

6 **7** 8 9 10 11 12 13 14 15 16 17 18 19 20

9 + 6 = ☐

6 7 8 **9** 10 11 12 13 14 15 16 17 18 19 20

8 + 7 = ☐

6 7 **8** 9 10 11 12 13 14 15 16 17 18 19 20

3 (Circle) the two numbers that add to 10. Add the next number.

10

5 + 3 + **5** = 10 + 3 = 13

10

6 + 2 + **4** = ☐ + ☐ = ☐

4 + 7 + 3 = ☐ + ☐ = ☐

8 + 5 + 2 = ☐ + ☐ = ☐

3 + 6 + 7 = ☐ + ☐ = ☐

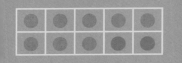
51	52	53	54	55	56	57	58	59	60
61	62	63	64	65	66	67	68	69	70
71	72	73	74	75	76	77	78	79	80
81	82	83	84	85	86	87	88	89	90

④ Jump to the nearest ten, then add the difference.

59 + 7 ⟶ 60 + 6 = ☐

68 + 6 ⟶ 70 + ☐ = ☐

77 + 7 ⟶ ☐ + ☐ = ☐

56 + 8 ⟶ ☐ + ☐ = ☐

67 + 5 ⟶ ☐ + ☐ = ☐

75 + 8 ⟶ ☐ + ☐ = ☐

58 + 5 ⟶ ☐ + ☐ = ☐

Mathseeds First Grade Workbook

5 ✏️ Bridge to ten to find the answers.

Dizzy cooks 9 carrots. Mango cooks 8 more.
How many altogether? _____

Doc has 17 marbles. Dizzy gives him 8 more.
How many altogether? _____

Ruby buys 58 beads. Doc finds 8 more.
How many altogether? _____

Waldo has 29 fish. He catches 6 more.
How many altogether? _____

I finished this lesson online.	This pet hatched.	I can	Driving tests
 96	Emilio the _____	• Bridge to a ten, then add the difference ☐	Tick when complete. Operations 18: Make 10 to add ☐

1 ✏️ Write the numbers for these tally marks.

卌 || _____   卌 卌 _____ ||\\ _____

2 ✏️ Draw the tally marks for these numbers.

5 _____   8 _____   4 _____

3 ✏️ Complete Doc's table. Give the table a title.

Foods	**Tally marks**	**Total**
Cereal	卌 ||\\	
Toast		7
Fruit	卌	
Yogurt		3

4 ✏️ Use Doc's table to complete the picture graph.

Cereal	🥣	🥣	🥣						
Toast	🍞								
Fruit	🍓								
Yogurt	🥛								

The Zoo

⑤ ✏ Complete the data table.

Animals	Tally marks	Total
Zebra		
Elephant		
Lizard		
Duck		

⑥ ✏ Answer the questions.

Which animal is there most of? _____

Which animal is there least of? _____

7 ✏️ Turn this data table into a picture graph.

Banana	Apple	Cherry	Watermelon
8	3	2	5

Title:

2				
1				
	🍎	🍒	🍌	🍉

8 ✏️ Answer the questions.

Which fruit is there most of? _____

Which fruit is there least of? _____

Which fruit is there five of? _____

Favorite Shapes

10			■	
9			■	
8	●		■	
7	●		■	
6	●		■	
5	●	▲	■	
4	●	▲	■	▬
3	●	▲	■	▬
2	●	▲	■	▬
1	●	▲	■	▬

9 🖉 Answer the questions.

Which shape is most popular? _____

Which shape is least popular? _____

How many more squares than circles? _____

How many more squares than rectangles? _____

How many four-sided shapes altogether? _____

I finished this lesson online.

97

This pet hatched.

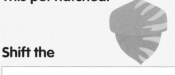

Shift the

I can
- Use tally marks to collect data ☐
- Use a picture graph to answer questions ☐

Driving tests
Tick when complete.
Data 10, 12, 15, 16:
Add all items
Order categories
Interpret a graph
Graph question

① Draw the tens and ones, then count to add.

$35 + 40 = \boxed{}$ $51 + 20 = \boxed{}$

Tens	Ones

Tens	Ones

② Draw the first number, then cross off the tens to subtract.

$89 - 50 = \boxed{}$ $64 - 30 = \boxed{}$

Tens	Ones

Tens	Ones

③ Find the answers.

$73 + 20 = \boxed{}$ $27 + 70 = \boxed{}$ $44 + 20 = \boxed{}$

$98 - 70 = \boxed{}$ $65 - 40 = \boxed{}$ $56 - 30 = \boxed{}$

Mathseeds First Grade Workbook

20 + 10 = ☐
20 − 10 = ☐

④ (Circle) the first number, then jump by tens.

61 + 30 = _____

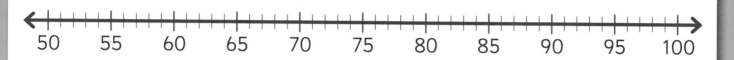

38 + 30 = _____

74 − 40 = _____

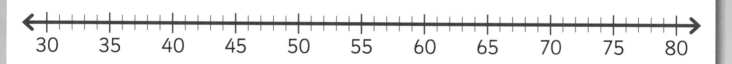

93 − 20 = _____

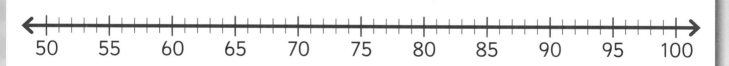

52 − 30 = _____

1	2	3	4	5	6	7	8	9	10
11	12	13	14	15	16	17	18	19	20
21	22	23	24	25	26	27	28	29	30
31	32	33	34	35	36	37	38	39	40
41	42	43	44	45	46	47	48	49	50
51	52	53	54	55	56	57	58	59	60
61	62	63	64	65	66	67	68	69	70
71	72	73	74	75	76	77	78	79	80
81	82	83	84	85	86	87	88	89	90
91	92	93	94	95	96	97	98	99	100

5 Jump up or down the hundred chart by tens to find the answers.

32 + 60 = ▢   56 + 20 = ▢   17 + 70 = ▢

95 − 80 = ▢   49 − 30 = ▢   84 − 50 = ▢

16 + 40 = ▢   25 + 50 = ▢   43 + 40 = ▢

91 − 50 = ▢   74 − 40 = ▢   37 − 20 = ▢

$20 + 10 =$
$20 - 10 =$

6 Find the answer. Show your working.

Ruby made 42 cookies and Dizzy made 50.

How many altogether?

Mango picked 71 berries but Waldo ate 40.

How many left?

Doc counted 58 circles and 30 triangles.

How many altogether?

Mango blew 86 bubbles but 60 popped.

How many left?

I finished this lesson online.	This pet hatched.	I can	Driving tests

Cecil the _____

I can
- Add and take away a group of tens
- Use different strategies to add and subtract

Driving tests
Tick when complete.
Operations 17, 19, 20:
Add tens to 2-digit
Add tens
Subtract tens

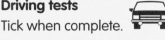

1 ✏️ Trace.

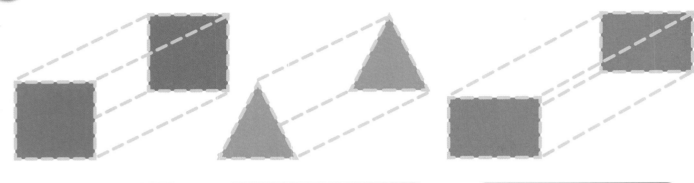

square prism   triangular prism   rectangular prism

2 Match the rectangular prisms to Dizzy and the triangular prisms to Mango.

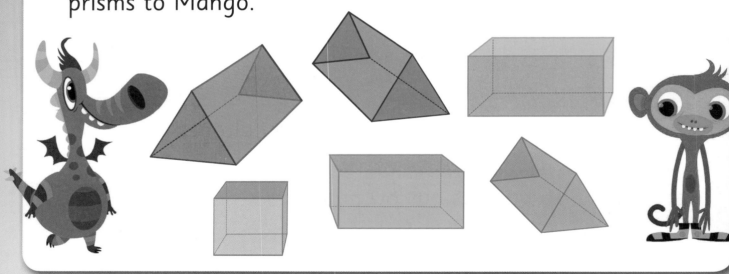

3 Circle the square prisms.

4 ✂ Cut out the pictures on page 259.
Paste them in the correct box.

square prism	triangular prism	rectangular prism

5 ✂ Cut out the labels on page 259.
Paste them next to the correct faces.

6 ✏️ Write the name of the shaded 2D face.

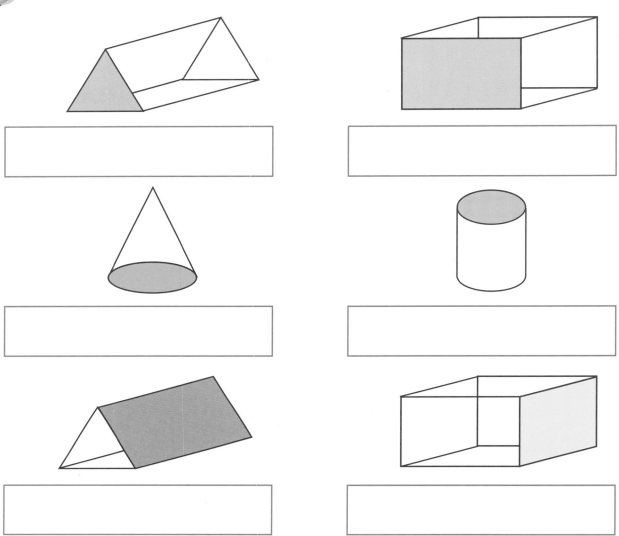

7 Color the shapes that make a square pyramid.

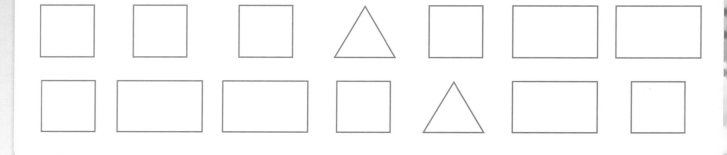

8 (Circle) the answers.

a Which shapes are the faces on a triangular prism?

rectangle   square   triangle   circle

b Which shapes are the faces on a rectangular prism?

rectangle   square   triangle   circle

9 Read and ✏ complete.

I have 2 ⬛ faces.   I have 2 🔺 faces.

I have 4 ▬ faces.   I have 3 ▬ faces.

I have 8 corners.   I have 6 corners.

I have 12 edges.   I have 9 edges.

I am a   I am a

_____.   _____.

Draw me.   Draw me.

Subtracting Unknown Numbers

1 ✏️ Take away the answer to find the missing number.
The first one is done for you.

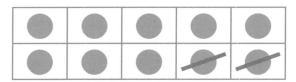 

$$15 - \boxed{8} = 7$$

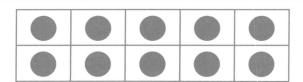 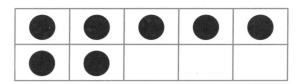

$$17 - \boxed{} = 6$$

$$14 - \boxed{} = 9$$

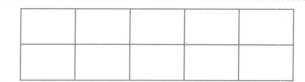 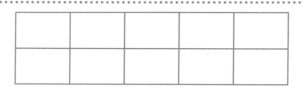

$$19 - \boxed{} = 8$$

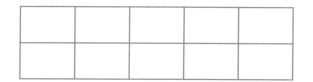 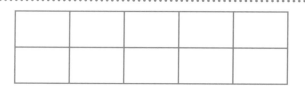

$$20 - \boxed{} = 4$$

2 ✏️ Make a number mountain.
The first one is done for you.

$9 - \boxed{} = 4$

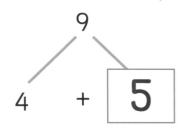

$10 - \boxed{} = 3$

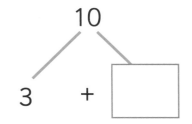

$11 - \boxed{} = 7$

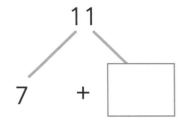

$15 - \boxed{} = 8$

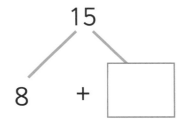

$19 - \boxed{} = 13$

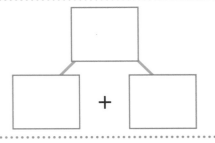

$17 - \boxed{} = 9$

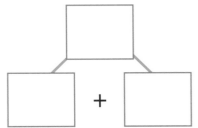

③ (Circle) the numbers and then count the difference.

$$18 - \boxed{} = 15$$

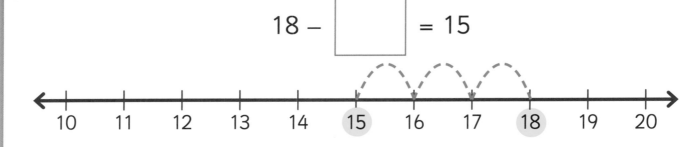

$$16 - \boxed{} = 14$$

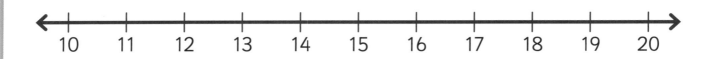

$$13 - \boxed{} = 11$$

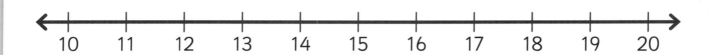

$$20 - \boxed{} = 12$$

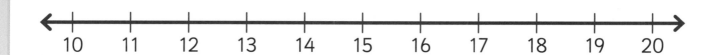

$$19 - \boxed{} = 13$$

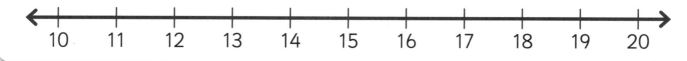

Mathseeds First Grade Workbook

4 Find the answers.  Show your working.

Ruby went shopping with
16 bags. She came home
with 11. How many bags
did she lose?

_____

Waldo took 13 fish cakes to
the picnic. He ate some on
the way and now has 7 left.
How many did he eat?

_____

Mango put 18 balls in a
bag. It had a hole and now
only 7 balls are in the bag.
How many fell out?

_____

Doc had 20 books. He gave
some to his friends and now
he has 14 left. How many
did he give away?

_____

I finished this lesson online.	This pet hatched.	I can	Driving tests
	Twitch the _____	• Use different strategies to find unknown numbers when subtracting ☐	Tick when complete. Operations 8: Complete the subtraction ☐

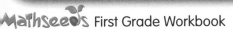

1 ✏️ Jump to the nearest ten, then add the difference.

$8 + 7 =$ $10 + 5 =$ ☐

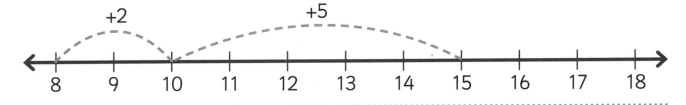

+2   +5

8 9 10 11 12 13 14 15 16 17 18

$17 + 6 =$ $20 +$ ☐ $=$ ☐

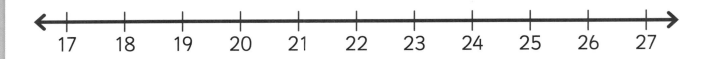

17 18 19 20 21 22 23 24 25 26 27

$29 + 5 =$ ☐ $+$ ☐ $=$ ☐

29 30 31 32 33 34 35 36 37 38 39

2 Find the answer. ✏️ Show your working.

Mango picked 57 bananas and 40 apples.

How many altogether?

3 Read the data table to answer the questions.

Favorite TV Shows			
Cartoons	Sport	Music	Cooking
10	7	5	2

How many people like sport shows best? _____

Which is the most popular type of show? _____

Which is the least popular type of show? _____

What is the difference between the number of people who like cartoons and music?

_____

4 Color the triangular prisms **red**, square prisms **yellow**, and rectangular prisms **green**.

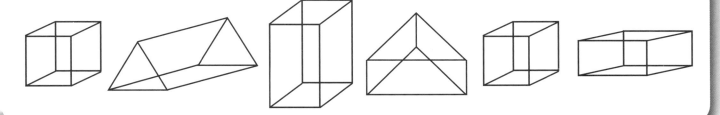

5 Find the answer. Show your working.

Doc has 19 books on his shelf.
He read some and has 7 books left.
How many books did he read?

_____

Excellent Work!

YOU COMPLETED

MAP 20

YOU CAN:

- [ ] **Bridge to a ten** when adding.
- [ ] **Add groups of ten**.
- [ ] Use a **data table** to answer questions.
- [ ] Recognize square prisms, triangular prisms, and rectangular **prisms**.
- [ ] Use different stategies to find an **unknown number when subtracting**.

Signed:

_____

Dated:

1 ✏️ Complete the addition puzzle.

1	−		=	0
+		+		

	+	4	=	8

| = | | = | | + |

3	+		=	5		5

| + | | | | | | = |

| 6 | | 5 | + | | = | 10 |

| = |

| | + | 10 | = | 18 |

2 Put the numbers into the machine. ✏️ Write each answer.

6
10
23
47 → +10 →

✏️ Draw your own number machine that **takes away 10**.
Write each answer.

1 Are these sums equal? Color yes or no.

12 = 14 − 2 (yes) (no)   15 − 5 = 10 (yes) (no)

18 − 9 = 8 (yes) (no)   14 = 20 − 6 (yes) (no)

2 Count and complete.

| 2s | 2 | 4 | ___ | ___ | 10 | ___ | 14 | 16 | 18 |

| 5s | 5 | ___ | ___ | 20 | 25 | ___ | 35 | ___ | ___ |

3 (Circle) the hens facing left. ✗Cross out the hens facing right.

4 Continue counting by 10s.

(10) (20) ( ) ( ) (50) ( ) ( ) (80) ( ) (100)

5 Count the length. Label them **longer** or **shorter**.

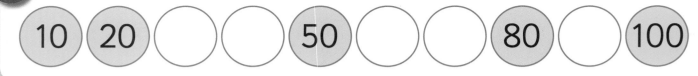

6 Count the tally marks. Write the number.

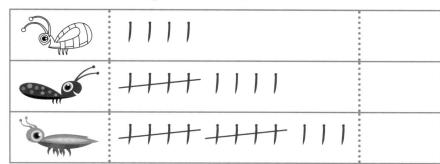

🐛						
🪲	┼┼┼┼					
🦗	┼┼┼┼ ┼┼┼┼				

How many bugs altogether? ☐

7 Color the correct answer.

It will rain next week.

(will happen)

(might happen)

Cats will grow wings and fly.

(will happen)

(won't happen)

8 Find the total cost.

$4 $3

☐ + ☐ = ☐

How much change from $10?

☐ − ☐ = ☐

9 Use the number line to bridge 10.

17 + 6 = ☐

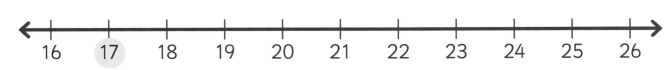

16 17 18 19 20 21 22 23 24 25 26

10 Match.

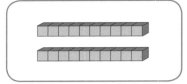

ten
20
30
forty
50
sixty
70
80
ninety
100

thirty

eighty

fifty

seventy

tens	ones
9	0

tens	ones
6	0

11 Use the number line to find the difference.

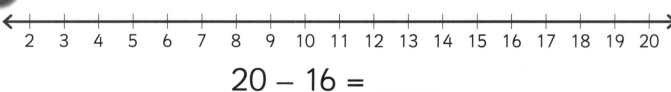

$$20 - 16 = \underline{\qquad}$$

12 Match.

 object
 name
 faces

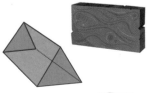

triangular prism

rectangular prism

square prism

 and

 and

Mathseeds First Grade Workbook

13 (Circle) the matching time.

14 Use near doubles to complete the sums.

☐ + ☐ + ☐ = ☐   ☐ + ☐ + ☐ = ☐

15 Complete the number fact family.

4 + ____ = 9   ____ − 5 = 4

5 + ____ = 9   9 − ____ = 5

16 Count on to add.

32 + 5 = ☐   34 + 6 = ☐

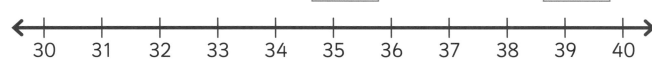

30   31   32   33   34   35   36   37   38   39   40

17 Add 5 more ones. Trade for a ten. Find the answer.

Tens	Ones

27 + 5 = ☐

Mathseeds

This is to certify that

_____

has completed the
Mathseeds
FIRST GRADE
Program

_____   _____

Date   Signature

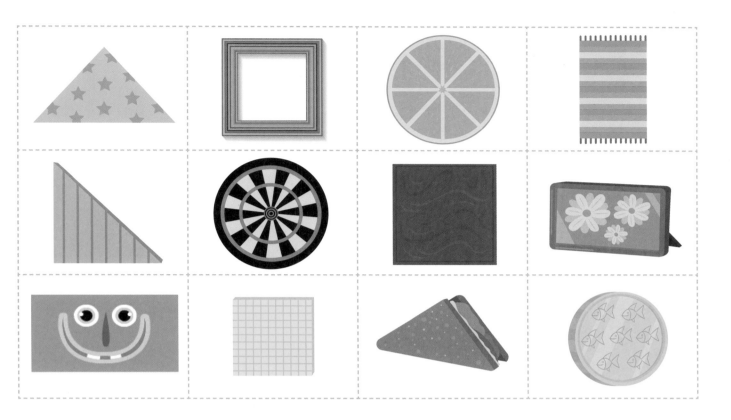

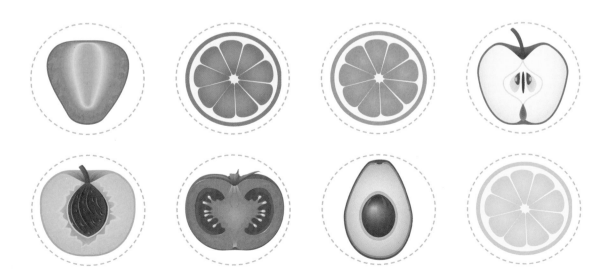

252

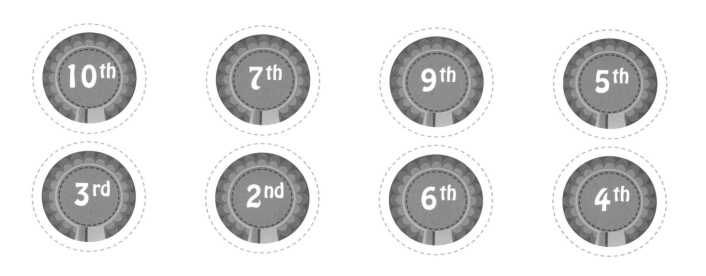

 page 87

✂ page 108

✂ page 140

78	79	
88	89	90
98	99	100

39	40
49	50
59	60

6	7	8	9	10
		18	19	20

31	32			
41	42	43	44	45

71			
81	82	83	84
91	92	93	94

Question 4

Question 5

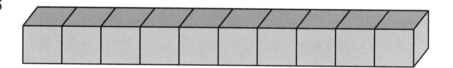

 page 192

Question 4

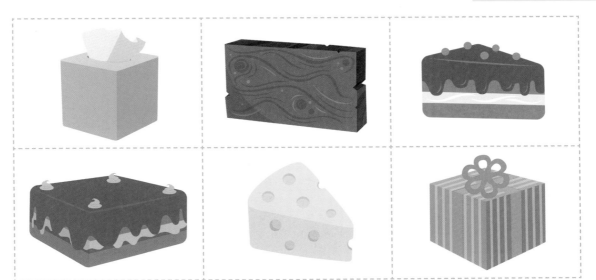

Question 5

square prism

rectangular prism

triangular prism

Mathseeds First Grade Workbook